Children's Picturebooks

The art of visual storytelling

Martin Salisbury with Morag Styles

Laurence King Publishing

LAURENCE KING

Published in 2012 by
Laurence King Publishing Ltd
361–373 City Road
London EC1V 1LR
United Kingdom
email: enquiries@laurenceking.com
www.laurenceking.com

Reprinted 2012 (twice)

A catalogue record for this book is available from the British Library

ISBN 978-1-85669-738-5

Design: Studio Ten and a Half
Cover art: Beatrice Alemagna
Research assistant: Pam Smy
Book photography: Ida Riveros

Printed in China

Contents

Introduction

It is often said that we live in an increasingly visual, image-based culture. The digital age has brought with it a growing expectation of pictorial instruction, signs and symbols. Images, moving or static, now seem to accompany most forms of information and entertainment. The art of illustration is traditionally defined as one of elucidating or decorating textual information by augmenting it with visual representation. But in many contexts the image has begun to replace the word. An iconic image of a rubbish bin now says, 'Do you want to throw this away?'

The picturebook as it is today is a relatively new form. We may debate its true origins but it is only 130 years or so since Randolph Caldecott began to elevate the role of the image in the narrative. Today's picturebook is defined by its particular use of sequential imagery, usually in tandem with a small number of words, to convey meaning. In contrast to the illustrated book, where pictures enhance, decorate and amplify, in the picturebook the visual text will often carry much of the narrative responsibility. In most cases, the meaning emerges through the interplay of word and image, neither of which would make sense when experienced independently of the other. It is a form that continues to evolve, and is being stretched and challenged by an increasingly experimental body of 'makers' (a suitable term for the artist–author of the picturebook has yet to be found). This evolution sometimes seems to be happening too fast for a world that has grown up expecting pictures to play a subordinate role in storytelling. Many adults who come into contact with the form as parents, teachers or reviewers will be educated primarily in verbal rather than visual literature. It is still common to see reviews of picturebooks that nervously venture 'beautifully illustrated' as a footnote.

Of course, the word 'picturebook' is usually preceded by the word 'children's'. But once again, this assumption about the form is being challenged. Traditionally, it has been regarded as a stepping stone to accepted notions of literacy for three- to seven-year-olds. There is no doubt that this is indeed one important role of the picturebook. However, as its audience and its reach widen, and we see the art of picturebook-making increasingly crossing over with the book arts, a new understanding of this hybrid art form will perhaps begin to emerge.

At university level, interest in and research around the subject of the picturebook has tended to divide clearly between the practitioners in the art and design sector and the theorists in the education sector. Between us, we represent both of these worlds and have for a number of years sought to build links between the two, jointly supervising research students and bringing our respective masters students together to learn from each other. In this book, we have also sought to bring together the practice and theory of children's picturebook illustration in an accessible and insightful way.

In the following chapters we explore not only the history and evolution of the picturebook, but all aspects of the 'art' of picturebook-making – from education and training to the interplay of words and images on a page, from the use of old and new printing methods to the editorial process and the demands of the publishing industry in the twenty-first century. As part of this exploration, we also examine the role of the picturebook in introducing children to the visual arts as well as language, and consider important issues such as the appropriateness of certain subjects and styles of illustration for children. We look, too, at the picturebook in the classroom. Here, we draw on the critical theory of scholars, such as Barbara Bader, and in particular on the research of Evelyn Arizpe and Morag Styles.

The picturebook maker's art is also explored through professional and student case studies at the end of each chapter. These studies, based on interviews with artists, students and publishers (which took place in 2009 and 2010), look in more detail at topics and issues raised in the chapters, and provide valuable information and inspiration for students studying picturebook illustration.

Above all, *Children's Picturebooks* is intended as a celebration of an art form that we believe to be deserving of greater recognition, both as art and as literature – *visual* literature.

Martin Salisbury and Morag Styles, 2012

Opposite: Anca Sandu, 2010.

A BRIEF HISTORY OF THE PICTURE BOOK

Early precursors

The history of the modern picturebook, as we have defined it, is relatively short but to track its evolution it may help to take a very brief look at the broader history of illustrated books for children. Of course, pictorial storytelling can be traced back as far as the earliest paintings on cave walls, which would have been gazed upon and enjoyed by people of all ages. Some of the examples in France and Spain may be 30,000–60,000 years old. We can only speculate as to the purpose or meaning of this art, but the images would have been one of the most important means of communication at the time – and continued to be so long after the arrival of the spoken and written word in the earliest civilizations.

Trajan's Column in Rome is often cited as one of the oldest examples of visual narrative, depicting as it does in great detail the story of Trajan's victories in the Dacian Wars at the start of the second century AD. The frieze winds its way up the column intricately describing the stories of the various battles in carved relief. The tombs of ancient Egypt and the walls of Pompeii are

Below: Mankind has felt the need to communicate through pictures for thousands of years. Scholars have speculated as to the purpose of early cave paintings but their sheer beauty is self-evident.

also evidence of our long-standing need to describe and communicate through pictures the world as we experience it.

The oldest surviving illustrated book is said to be an Egyptian papyrus roll of around 1980 BC. The pure chance of its survival, buried in sand, suggests that such artefacts had been around for much longer. It is thought that words and pictures were inscribed on to perishable materials such as wood, leaves, leather and early forms of paper in many ancient cultures. David Bland, in *The Illustration of Books* (Faber, 1951), speculates that the ancient Chinese ideogram:

… which is a picture of the thing it represents, is one of the first forms of illustration and it is difficult to conceive of a closer relationship between text and illustration than such a combination as that.

Bland's later and more substantial work, *A History of Book Illustration* (Faber, 1958), is an invaluable, scholarly examination of the origins and evolution of the illustrated book, from ancient civilizations through the medieval illuminated manuscript to the birth of print. The quotation attributed to the fifteenth-century painter and sculptor Leonardo da Vinci, with which Bland opens the book, seems particularly apposite in relation to our interest here – the modern picturebook:

And you who wish to represent by words the form of man and all the aspects of his membrification, relinquish that idea. For the more minutely you describe the more you will confine the mind of the reader, and the more you will keep him from the knowledge of the thing described. And so it is necessary to draw and to describe.

Below: The intensely detailed narrative illustrations on Trajan's Column give a pictorial account of the wars between the Romans and the Dacians. The stories are told through relief carvings on a frieze that winds around the column 23 times.

The printing of books from the fifteenth to the nineteenth century

The invention of printing in the fifteenth century meant that education in the West began to become available to more than just the wealthy few who had access to hand-produced literature. Most scholars agree that printing, like paper, originated in China. Block printing had certainly been around for a while but in Europe it was the invention of movable type by Johannes Gutenberg in the 1430s that opened the way for viable mass publishing.

Ulrich Boner's *Der Edelstein* (1461) is often cited as the first example of a book with type and image printed together. Comenius' *Orbis Sensualium Pictus* (The Visible World), published in Nuremberg in 1658, is generally seen as the first children's picturebook, in the sense that it was a book of pictures designed for children to read. It is not until much later that the precursors of the picturebook as we know it begin to emerge. The chapbooks of the sixteenth to the nineteenth century were cheaply produced, illustrated with crudely prepared and printed woodcuts and were hawked around the

Right: William Blake's integration of words and images within a pictorial whole is often seen as an early forerunner of today's picturebook. This frontispiece for *Songs of Innocence and of Experience* would not look out of place as a title page in a modern children's picturebook.

Below: The term 'chapbook' derives from 'chapman', the word used to describe a pedlar who hawked the books around the country along with his other wares. The pocket-sized books contained woodcut prints such as this one, rather randomly related to a text.

countryside by pedlars for an audience with often limited levels of literacy and funds. The relationship between words and pictures here was often a tenuous and largely decorative one.

The inspirational painter and poet William Blake can, perhaps, be seen as the first to experiment with the symbiotic relationship between word and image, at least in the sense of their visual arrangement. Blake produced *Songs of Innocence* in 1789, printing and publishing the book himself. His idiosyncratic, visionary visual style was totally original, and owed little to anything that was happening in the visual arts at that time. Brian Alderson, in his book *Sing a Song for Sixpence: The English Picture Book Tradition and Randolph Caldecott* (Cambridge University Press, 1986), declares succinctly:

So it comes about that the first masterpiece of English children's literature, which is also the first great original picture book, stems from an impulse to integrate words and images within a single linear whole.

Thomas Bewick's emergence in the late eighteenth century must be mentioned in relation to the general development of book illustration because of his achievement in elevating the art of wood engraving to a completely new level. His technical skills – engraving in fine line on the end grain of dense woods such as box – combined with an intense interest in the natural world produced results that took the process way beyond a merely reprographic role. The central character of one of the earliest depictions of a believable child in literature, in chapter one of *Jane Eyre* by Charlotte Brontë (first published in 1847 by Smith, Elder & Co), finds comfort in looking at Bewick's artwork.

Left: Thomas Bewick's engravings introduced new levels of technique and an earthy anecdotal charm to the world of book illustration.

Colour printing in the nineteenth century

Until the 1830s colour was usually added by hand until a process for printing colour from woodblocks was invented, independently of each other, by George Baxter and Charles Knight. Baxter patented his 'Baxter process', which combined an intaglio keyplate with multiple woodblocks, in 1835. An Austrian, Aloysius Senefelder, had invented the principle of lithography (which is the basis of all mass printing today) in the late eighteenth century, but it would be a while before the process was in regular use.

One of the more direct influences on the modern picturebook is *Der Struwwelpeter* by Heinrich Hoffmann. Much has been made of the levels of cruelty and violence in Hoffmann's cautionary tales of the ghastly consequences of misbehaviour but they have stood the test of time in every sense, having been reinterpreted through many and varying media. The original title, *Funny Stories and Droll Pictures*, hints at a playful, even ironic intent on the part of the author that presages the contemporary postmodern picturebook. Hoffmann's famous book reached England from Germany in around 1848, and is comparable in many ways to Edward Lear's *A Book of Nonsense* which had been published just a couple of years before. But while there are stylistic parallels, heightened by the printing processes of the time, Lear's delightfully anarchic visual and verbal texts show no inclination to moralize, or indeed to conform, to any rules of linear narrative. If any meaning can be ascribed in the traditional sense, it may be the championing of the outsider, perhaps as a consequence of Lear's recurrent bouts of depression.

Right: Edward Lear's illustrations to his *A Book of Nonsense* were in stark contrast to his topographical travel paintings. As a travelling watercolourist, Lear depicted panoramic landscapes with subtle washes. To accompany his nonsense limericks he created playfully anarchic line drawings that perfectly echo his words.

There was an Old Man of Corfu,
Who never knew what he should do;
So he rushed up and down, till the sun made him brown,
That bewildered Old Man of Corfu.

The birth of the modern picturebook in the late nineteenth century

It was at exactly the time of the publication of *A Book of Nonsense* that the most important figure in the picturebook's evolution was born. Randolph Caldecott is generally acknowledged to be the father of the picturebook. Maurice Sendak, perhaps the greatest author of visual literature of our time, identifies Caldecott's place in the picturebook pantheon. Writing in his book of essays, *Caldecott & Co: Notes on Books and Pictures* (Farrar, Straus & Giroux, 1988), he explains:

Caldecott's work heralds the beginning of the modern picture book. He devised an ingenious juxtaposition of picture and word, a counterpoint that never happened before. Words are left out – but the picture says it. Pictures are left out – but the word says it. In short, it is the invention of the picture book.

This 'rhythmic syncopation', as Sendak describes it, was a radical departure from the relationship between the visual and verbal texts that had prevailed hitherto. In stories such as *A Frog he would A-wooing Go* (George Routledge & Sons, 1883) and *Come Lasses and Lads* (George Routledge & Sons, 1884) a pictorial subtext emerges that expands rather than merely duplicates or decorates the narrative content as conveyed by the written word. Caldecott's superlative draughtsmanship, of course, seals his position in the history of picturebooks. The

Below and opposite: Randolph Caldecott's 'picture books' broke new ground in expanding the role of the image in relation to text; they liberated artists to augment words with additional, visual meaning.

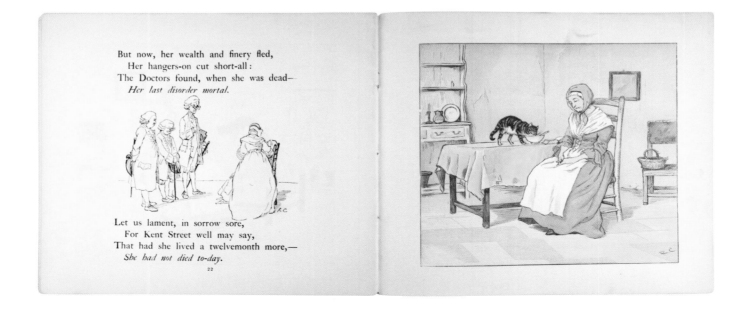

But now, her wealth and finery fled,
  Her hangers-on cut short-all:
The Doctors found, when she was dead—
  Her last disorder mortal.

Let us lament, in sorrow sore,
  For Kent Street well may say,
That had she lived a twelvemonth more,—
  She had not died to-day.

22

books were published as *Randolph Caldecott's Picture Books* and Caldecott is thought to have been the first artist to negotiate a royalty payment (one penny per book) rather than a flat fee.

Caldecott tends to be bracketed with two other artists of the mid to late Victorian era: Walter Crane and Kate Greenaway. Though their work is in many ways very different to Caldecott's, it is linked to his picturebooks by the key role played in its dissemination by the printer Edmund Evans. At this time the distinction between printer and publisher had not really emerged. Evans brought a sophisticated eye to the works of these three artists and the best way to do justice to them in mass reproduction. The garish and oily effects of the chromolithographic processes that prevailed were not sympathetic or appealing to the better artists of the day. Evans, an artist himself, demonstrated that colour printing with wood could be subtle, effective and cheap. He pioneered the application of photographic processes to the preparation of woodblocks.

Walter Crane's work demonstrates a preoccupation with the visual, rather than the conceptual relationship between word and image, and is consequently much more static and less fluent than that of Caldecott. It has also come to embody in many ways the Arts and Crafts style. Crane's comments in his *Reminiscences* of 1907 on Evans' more 'tasteful' approach to printing are revealing: '… but it was not without protest from the publishers who thought the raw, coarse colours and vulgar designs usually current appealed to a larger public, and therefore paid better…'

Such tensions between perceptions of public taste/ commercial potential and artistic integrity are still hot topics of debate between artist and publisher today.

Kate Greenaway's fragrant, innocent world of *Under the Window* (George Routledge & Sons, 1879), with its distinctively prettily dressed children who looked like miniature adults, has survived the damnation of faint praise from contemporary and modern critics alike and her popularity endures. Alderson tells us that we, '… should not lose sight of the freshness of the little sub-fenestral world that Miss Greenaway brought to life' while reminding us of Beatrix Potter's blunt observation that 'she can't draw'.[1]

---

[1] Quoted by Brian Alderson, *Sing a Song for Sixpence: The English Picture Book Tradition and Randolph Caldecott*. Cambridge University Press, 1986.

The needy seldom pass'd her door,
And always found her kind;
She freely lent to all the poor—

7

From the golden age of illustration

The period during the latter half of the nineteenth and the early twentieth century has come to be known as the golden age of children's books, a time when there was a coming together of developments in printing technology, changing attitudes to childhood and the emergence of a number of brilliant artists. Sir John Tenniel's drawings for Lewis Caroll's *Alice's Adventures in Wonderland* (Macmillan, 1865) perhaps heralded this new age. They brought a new kind of presence on the page; the images played a key role in the experience of the book and, subsequently, became definitive to our reading of it.

With advances in photolithography, the intensely layered watercolour work of Arthur Rackham also came to the fore and the lavish gift-book tradition of the early twentieth century held sway. William Nicholson (later to become Sir William Nicholson) was at this time best known for his work with his brother-in-law, James Pryde, in poster design. In this field the two were known as the Beggerstaff Brothers, but Nicholson's distinctively bold use of black woodcut print with flat colour was cleverly

Below: William Nicholson is perhaps best known for his boldly designed linocut illustrations but *Clever Bill* is loosely rendered with line and colour separations and relaxed hand-rendered text.

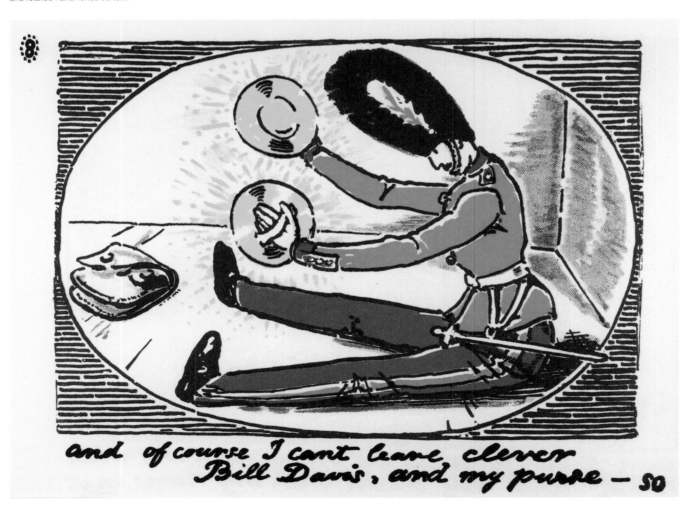

modified to pioneer the use of lithography in his later children's books, *Clever Bill* (Heinemann, 1926) and *The Pirate Twins* (Faber, 1929). These books are also important examples of what Alderson describes as a 'near perfect wedding of words and pictures into a unified whole' at a time when such integration was relatively rare.

In the early twentieth century experimentation with the art (and production) of the illustrated book was perhaps more adventurous and advanced in France than it was in Britain. The culture of the 'artist's book' was more firmly established there and, as a consequence, a wider range of printing processes was in use. While the letterpress line block dominated in Britain up to World War II, in France greater use was made not only of lithography but also of innovative processes such as *pochoir*, a technique that involved hand-colouring through stencils (see p. 156). Edy Legrand's *Macao et Cosmage* was produced in this way in 1919 (Nouvelle Revue Française); the black line was printed lithographically and the other colours were stencilled.

This large square-format production provided a sumptuous but relatively cheap alternative to the average mass-produced book of the time. Ten years later in Britain, Edward McKnight Kauffer used the *pochoir* process in his illustrations to Arnold Bennett's *Elsie and the Child*, published in a limited edition by Cassell.

Below: A natural sense of placement and an elegant relationship between line and flat colour characterize Edy Legrand's *Macao et Cosmage*. The hand-rendered art deco type is highly evocative of the period.

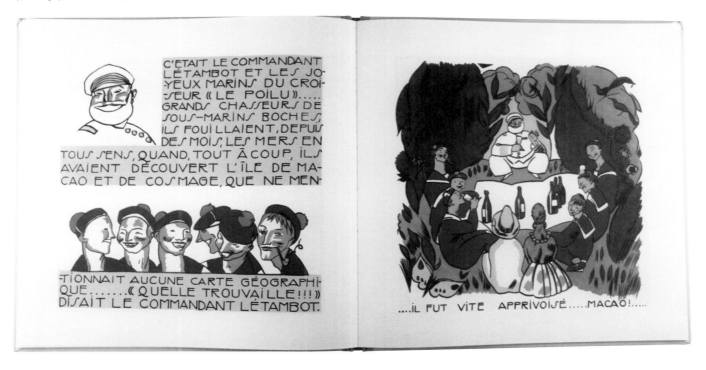

The 1930s

Babar the elephant made his first appearance with *The Story of Babar* in 1931, published in France by Condé Nast. He was the creation of Jean de Brunhoff, a painter from Paris whose father was a publisher. The books were like nothing seen before, with their large, colourful format and handwritten text rendered with a simple, childlike clarity. In Britain the books were published by Methuen and printed by one of the most important quality printing houses at this time: W.S. Cowell of Ipswich. Jean de Brunhoff created another five Babar titles before his untimely death from tuberculosis in 1937. His son, Laurent, was only twelve at the time. After World War II, Laurent decided to continue his father's work and went on to create further Babar books over many decades and into the twenty-first century.

The original Babar books have divided sociopolitical commentators, some of whom argue that there are offensive, neocolonial aspects to the content, while others see a strong socialist ethic in the utopian milieu. Fellow artists, however,

Below: The de Brunhoffs' Babar, shown here in *Babar the King*, was an upright biped with little or no facial expression, but the books have proved
to have lasting value since their first appearance in 1931.

But what the elephants loved best of all

28

was the Theatre in the Palace of Pleasure.

29

have been generally unanimous in their praise. Maurice Sendak, contributing an introduction to *Babar's Anniversary Album* (Random House, 1981), observes that, 'Babar is at the very heart of my conception of what turns a picturebook into a work of art'. Laurent's version of Babar, while stylistically remarkably true to his father's original vision, leans more towards the fantastic in its subject matter.

By contrast, it would be difficult to read too much political or social agenda into the output of Edward Ardizzone. Ardizzone's work as an illustrator spanned much of the twentieth century, and he produced drawings for all age groups and all kinds of books. He was the consummate professional. Whatever the nature of the commission, he would bring the same charm and humanity to the drawings. A sense of affection for the various manifestations of the human condition, good or bad, shines through in all his books, without ever tipping over into the sentimental. His work is often described as quintessentially English: it reflects the particular architectural, rural and social

backdrops that played such a big part in his imagery, along with the gentility of manners of many of his characters.

As far as the picturebook is concerned, Ardizzone's *Little Tim* books hold a key place in the evolution of the genre. The first of these, *Little Tim and the Brave Sea Captain*, was published in 1936 by Oxford University Press. The *Tim* stories were initially produced in a large 9 × 13 in (230 × 330 mm) format, and printed in full colour throughout – but only on one side of the paper. Later, the books became smaller and the colour illustrations were interspersed with black-and-white drawings. For the colour illustrations, Ardizzone drew the black ink line on a separate, transparent overlay while the watercolour washes were painted on another sheet of paper. This tricky process was the only way to achieve a solid printed black line that matched his original, rather than one that was made up of a combination of the other three colours of the lithographic process: magenta, cyan and yellow. The *Tim* books combine a relaxed, hand-drawn font with atmospheric

Below: Edward Ardizzone's *Tim* books have been reissued many times. The originals, such as *Tim to the Rescue* (Oxford, 1949), shown here, were superbly printed and free of any political correctness.

illustrations of wildly improbable texts that still appeal today to a child's yearning for adventure and independence.

Mervyn Peake was one of the more imaginative and original artists to emerge in the 1930s, through both his visual and verbal texts. *Captain Slaughterboard Drops Anchor* was his first picturebook and was initially developed while Peake was still in his twenties. It was published in 1939 by Country Life shortly before the outbreak of World War II. The initial response of critics to the less than cosy and somewhat decadent world of pirates and alien creatures was lukewarm. *Punch* magazine declared it to be 'quite unsuitable for sensitive children'. Soon there were remaindered copies for sale at two shillings and sixpence. But then the whole stock was destroyed by fire when the warehouse in which the books were stored was bombed by the Luftwaffe. A rare 1939 first edition is now one of the most collectable and expensive of children's books. *Captain Slaughterboard* was reprinted at the end of the war in 1945 and published by Eyre and Spottiswoode, this time with coloured tints added by Peake. The paper was of typically poor post-war quality so surviving copies of this edition are also much sought after. The poetry of Mervyn Peake's creation and the subtle interplay of word and image on the page make this a key picturebook that was way ahead of its time.

As the 1930s drew to a close and war enveloped Europe, what was to become one of the most popular characters in American picturebooks was emerging in the minds of its authors. *Curious George* was first published in 1941 (Houghton Mifflin), after an epic journey to New York by his creators Margaret and H.A. Rey. The couple escaped war-torn Europe, carrying the manuscript for the first book with them. The tailless George is an amalgam of monkey, ape and child. In the first book he is brought from the jungle by a character known simply as 'the man in the yellow hat'. Despite, or perhaps because of, these eccentricities, George's popularity as a character led to eight books, the last of which was published in the mid-1960s, his appeal reaching across the globe.

Below: Mervyn Peake's highly eccentric *Captain Slaughterboard Drops Anchor* was reprinted in this newly coloured edition by Walker Books in 2001. As well as illustration, Peake's interests ranged across painting, writing and theatre.

Puffin Picture Books, autolithography and the European influence

The editor, designer and publisher Noel Carrington was a well-known figure in London publishing in the 1930s. Through his work for Country Life, an imprint owned by George Newnes, he was experienced in collaborating with artists to prepare illustrations for reproduction. In this capacity he had been instrumental in the publishing of *High Street* (1938), a key twentieth-century illustrated book, about shopfronts, illustrated with exquisite lithographs by Eric Ravilious.

Carrington had the idea of producing affordable educational picturebooks for children, with high-quality artwork and in a format that could be printed in large numbers. In 1938 he put his ideas to Allen Lane, who had recently launched the Penguin Books series. Crucial to the idea was the proposal that artists would draw directly on to lithographic plates, creating a separate drawing for each of the colours to be printed, thereby saving a great deal of money on photographic colour separation. This process of the very direct involvement of artist and printer was referred to as autolithography. Despite the outbreak of war the Puffin Picture Books series went ahead.

The format of the books was important to the cost-saving ethos of the project. The 32 pages, each in a 7 × 9 in (180 × 230 mm) format, were created by printing the entire book on one large sheet of paper, colour on one side, black and white on the other. When folded and trimmed, this gave a complete book with alternate colour and black-and-white spreads. They were printed by W.S. Cowell of Ipswich.

Carrington was aware of the use of the autolithography process in other European countries in the preceding years, including a similar series which he had seen in Russia. In France, the Flammarion Père Castor storybooks had also been lithographed in this way. The Puffin Picture Books were a runaway success and continued to be produced in vast numbers through the 1940s, 1950s and 1960s. Among the artists who showed the greatest skill in translating their work through the medium of autolithography were Stanley Badmin, Clarke Hutton, Kathleen Hale and Edward Bawden. Bawden's *The Arabs* (Puffin, 1947) is a superb production, now highly collectable, which was informed by the artist's recent experience of the Middle East as an official war artist.

Carrington's passion for quality illustration, and his keen eye for talent, continued to play an important role in the development of the picturebook in Britain. Books published in the Puffin series, and also by imprints such as Transatlantic Arts and Country Life, continued to exploit the process of autolithography. A particularly important discovery was Kathleen Hale, whose *Orlando's Camping Holiday* and *Orlando's Trip Abroad* Carrington published in 1938 and 1939. Hale taught herself the process of lithography, and became a master of the subtleties of colour separation. She worked initially on grained metal plates, later on the plastic sheets known as Plasticowell that W.S. Cowell developed. The adventures of Orlando the marmalade cat became twentieth-century classics. Hale was one of the first to recognize the importance of appealing to an adult audience as well as to the child. She included little humorous visual and verbal asides that were clearly designed to amuse the adult who would be required to read the stories over and over again.

Below: Eric Ravilious' lithographic illustrations to *High Street* have made the book one of the most sought after and collectable twentieth-century illustrated books. Its successful use of autolithography encouraged publisher Noel Carrington to develop the Puffin Picture Books.

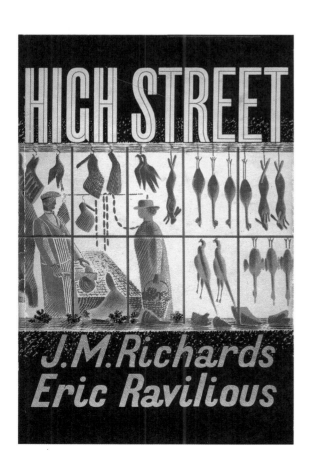

Left: Edward Bawden's illustrations to *The Arabs* by R.B. Serjeant were a highlight of the Puffin Picture series. Bawden successfully combined a mechanical approach to architecture and perspective with a subtle lightness of touch.

Below: Kathleen Hale's *Orlando* books have achieved classic status. Her distinctively grainy graphite colour separations are among the most memorable in the Puffin Picture series. From *Orlando's Invisible Pyjamas*.

"Now it's MY turn!" said Tinkle. "I drump I had a lorry-load of ice-cream—that's all and can I have a shilling please?" he asked Orlando.

"You can have tuppence," said Orlando smiling.

"Huh. *That's* not much to help me on my grownup way," grumbled Tinkle.

The dreams were soon told and Orlando began to worry about himself again.

20

Tinkle was sorry for him, and ashamed of grumbling; he wanted to please Orlando more than ever.

"Tell us a story of your yoof," he suggested, for he knew that people liked nothing better than to talk about themselves.

"A story of my youth?" replied Orlando. "Well, if you bring me the family photograph album, the pictures will remind me of things."

21

The time came when Grace wanted to wash the pyjamas. Sadly Orlando went back to bed and took them off. To his surprise, instead of finding his naked flesh, there appeared to be another pair of pyjamas covering him.

"How clever of you Grace, to have made a lining... I needn't stay in bed after all!"

"A lining?" replied Grace puzzled, "That's no lining" she cried with delight, "that's your own fur which has grown at last!"

The cats were too happy to speak; they purred loudly until they sneezed.

28

Orlando decided to present the pyjamas to the Anti-Fur-Trappers' League, for their museum to show people how lovely imitation fur can be.

The Presentation of the Invisible Pyjamas took place in the Town Hall, and the building was crowded. There were long and eloquent speeches, during which Orlando and Grace sat modestly in the limelight.

29

Left: Enid Marx was a designer, illustrator and writer of books on the popular arts. She is perhaps best known for her fabric and poster designs for London Transport. *The Little White Bear* was published by Faber in 1945. Three colour separations were drawn directly on to the lithographic plate and printed on a textured paper.

Below: Stanley Badmin's mastery of the autolithographic process was matched by his knowledge of the English landscape. His work was often credited as S.R. Badmin.

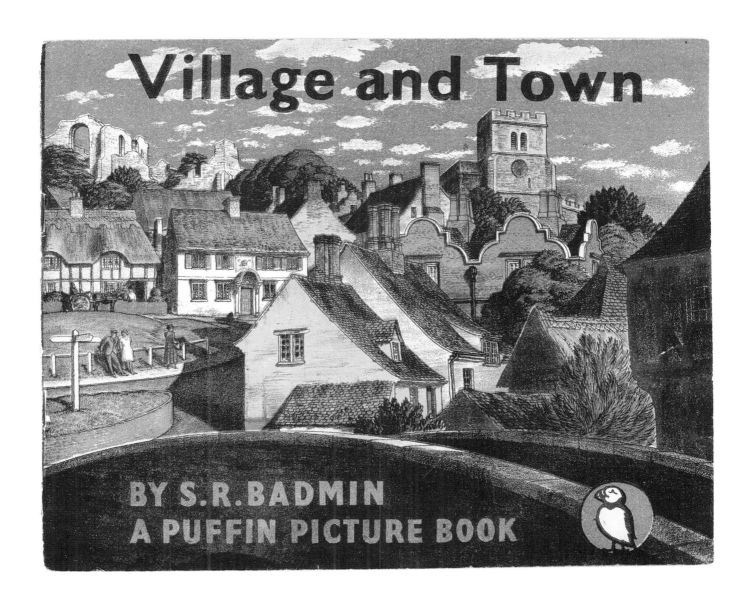

The post-war years

As Europe emerged from war, the need to keep publishing costs low was greater than ever, and shortages meant many books were printed on poor-quality paper. Autolithography continued to be a popular means of production and Noel Carrington's influence in Britain continued. Through the Transatlantic Arts imprint he introduced artists such as Susan Einzig, a German-Jewish refugee who had been one of the last Jews to escape Nazi Germany. Under her original name, Susanne Einzig, she illustrated the charming little *Mary Belinda and the Ten Aunts* (text by Norah Pulling, Transatlantic Arts, 1950). Einzig would go on to be an important artist, perhaps best known for her illustrations to Philippa Pearce's *Tom's Midnight Garden* (Oxford University Press, 1958).

Other examples of the autolithographed picturebook include *Ballet in England: A Book of Lithographs* by Sheila Jackson (Transatlantic Arts, 1945) and *The Little White Bear* written and illustrated by Enid Marx (Faber & Faber, 1945). In America, many charming books were produced by the husband and wife team

Below and right: Transatlantic Arts produced a number of highly individual and beautifully illustrated picturebooks. *Mary Belinda and the Ten Aunts* by Norah Pulling featured illustrations by a young Susan Einzig, who later recalled the luxury of having a team of skilled lithographers at her disposal at Cowell printers.

Opposite: *The Little Red Engine Goes to Town* (text Diana Ross; Faber & Faber, 1952) featured illustrations by Leslie Wood, an artist who worked mainly in advertising and who took over from the Polish duo, Lewitt-Him. This title featured the Festival of Britain.

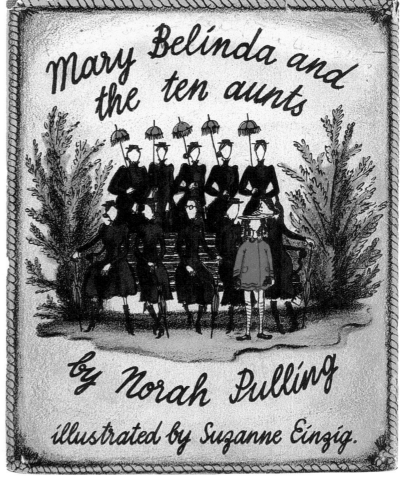

Ingri and Edgar Parin d'Aulaire, who met as art students in Munich in the 1920s and emigrated to the United States in 1925. Worth a mention here, too, are the *Little Red Engine* books, some of which were produced through autolithography. The original illustrations to these popular stories by Diana Ross were produced by Lewitt-Him, the design partnership made up of Jan Le Witt and George Him who had arrived in England from their native Poland in 1937. Much of their graphic work was to be in the field of poster and advertising design. The *Little Red Engine* illustrations are a fascinating fusion of a clearly eastern European graphic tradition and deeply English subject matter. Later editions of the series were illustrated by Leslie Wood.

Alongside the austerity and paper shortages that prevailed in the early post-war years, there was a yearning for colour and escape that manifested itself in the arts in what became known as the neo-romantic movement. In Britain there was a short-lived period of romantic and narrative painting, rooted in the spirit of landscape and a need to reassert a sense of belonging to the land. With the benefit of hindsight, many cultural commentators have described this period as inward-looking and regressive. It was quickly overtaken by more strident movements in art and design, such as abstract expressionism, but it did have a particular impact on book illustration. A number of historically important illustrated books appeared in the late 1940s, featuring the work of leading artists of the time such as John Piper, Keith Vaughan and John Minton. In the field of children's books, Minton's illustrations to *The Snail That Climbed the Eiffel Tower*, a collection of indifferent short stories by Odo Cross for the influential publisher John Lehmann (1947), were perhaps the most notable example. Minton was a master of the letterpress line block and worked closely with the printer to utilize this process as a form of printmaking, carefully considering the effects of overlaying individual colour separations.

Below: Paul Rand's blurring of
boundaries between word and image
opened up new possibilities for the
language of the picturebook, as in these
spreads from *Sparkle and Spin*.

A word is a thing
you heard or saw
or can even draw a
picture of.
Words are the names of objects
like book and doll and chair
or of animals
like bird and dog and bear.

Words are "Yes I will"
and "No I won't,"
but they are polite too
like please and thank you.

The 1950s and visual thinking

From the 1950s an increasing number of graphic designers were drawn to the medium of the picturebook. This was a time when graphic design, illustration and painting were more closely related within art schools. Designers were trained in drawing and typography (and in drawing type). Suddenly, books that showed a unified approach to concept, image and typography were appearing, as many of their designers were also the authors. This is perhaps where the unique nature of the picturebook as a medium really began to assert itself. Now, words became fewer as an understanding of the potential of the page as a multimodal visual stage grew. And the English language picturebook benefited from the influence of a number of authorial artists of European or Latin origin who had been displaced by the war, or had arrived in the United States as immigrants. Among these were Antonio Frasconi, Roger Duvoisin, Leo Lionni and Miroslav Sasek.

The influential American graphic designer Paul Rand first ventured into the picturebook arena in a book written by his then wife, Ann Rand. *I Know a Lot of Things* was published by Harcourt Brace and World in 1956. It had been suggested to the legendary children's book editor Margaret McEldery that Rand's work would lend itself well to a children's book. A highly successful designer, he had begun to tire of, and question, the

Below: Antonio Frasconi's *See and Say* used bold print imagery to great effect to describe visually the meaning of words printed in four languages.

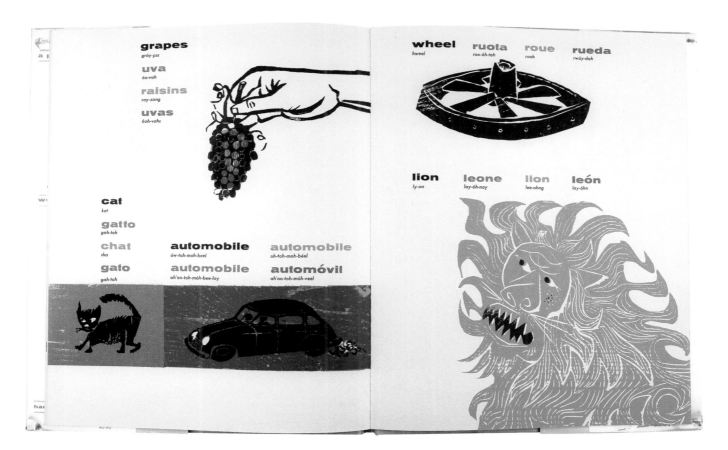

work he was doing in advertising and was looking for a more creatively (if not financially) rewarding area. There were three further books from the Rands, all with Harcourt Brace: *Sparkle and Spin* (1957), *Little 1* (1962) and *Listen! Listen!* (1970). All the books demonstrate a playful but sophisticated understanding of the relationship between words and pictures, shapes, sounds and thoughts.

Antonio Frasconi's ground-breaking *See and Say*, a simple concept that introduced children to a few words in four languages through the artist's characteristically bold yet gentle coloured woodcuts, appeared in 1955 (Harcourt Brace). Frasconi, who was born in Argentina and raised in Uruguay, moved to the United States in 1945. His work spanned the fine and applied arts and was often employed to expose political injustice.

Swiss-born Roger Duvoisin's artistic background was in theatre and textile design, and his skills in the latter took him from Europe to New York to take up a job with a textile firm. When the firm went out of business he concentrated on illustration.

The Happy Lion, the first in a highly successful series, appeared in 1954 and was written by his wife, Louise Fatio. Another highly successful animal character was Petunia the duck. Duvoisin's charming, gentle books won him numerous awards over a lengthy and prolific career.

Leo Lionni, who was brought up in Holland, Belgium, New York and Italy, is another key figure whose work in children's books emerged from a background in design in the late 1950s. But he came to this field relatively late after an early life full of changes of direction. As an adult, after trying a variety of careers, he moved to New York from Europe with his wife and children when war broke out and became a leading art director in advertising and magazines while also painting and exhibiting. Lionni's first, highly influential picturebook, *Little Blue and Little Yellow*, appeared in 1959 (Obolenski/Astor) at a time when he was tiring of the world of advertising. It has proved to have timeless appeal with its use of simple, torn paper shapes to describe how the friends, little blue and little yellow, are separated

Below: In *Little Blue and Little Yellow*, Leo Lionni used simple abstract shapes to explore the idea of relationships through colour.

Ils aiment jouer à cache-cache   et faire la ronde.

from each other. As they hug joyfully on being reunited, they turn to green. The book communicates on many levels; it is a simple introduction to colour and shapes but can also be read with reference to race and tolerance.

Of course, many of the best picturebook artists would not describe themselves exclusively as such. André François was born in Hungary, in an area that became part of Romania after World War I. But it was as a French citizen that he spent his working life as a graphic artist, spanning visual satire, advertising and poster design, theatre set design, sculpture and book illustration. François' work exhibited a childlike awkwardness that belied a highly sophisticated, biting eye. The first outlets he found for his work were British satirical magazines such as *Lilliput* and *Punch*. In children's books, François developed a successful partnership with the writer John Symonds, producing books such as *The Magic Currant Bun* (Faber, 1953) and *Tom et Tabby* (Delpire, 1963).

Below: André François' *Crocodile Tears* (Universe Books NY, 1956) uses an extreme landscape format to reflect and emphasize the subject matter. It was François' first picturebook as author–artist.

Needless to say, you have to get the correct measurements . . . not too long, not too short, or the crocodile will rattle about in the LONG CROCODILE BOX.

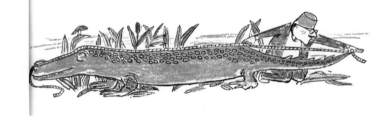

They take you on the lake on their backs

They can tell charming stories,

The 1960s

As the swinging sixties exploded into life, a number of British artists emerged from art school with work that heralded a new age of paint and colour in picturebooks. The shift was more than merely stylistic, however. As with developments in popular music, artists were beginning to express themselves in a more personal way; they were becoming the artistic equivalent of singer-songwriters. Among them were Brian Wildsmith, Charles Keeping, Raymond Briggs and John Burningham. Each of them would go on to lengthy and productive careers and make major contributions to the picturebook genre.

A key player in the careers of Wildsmith and Keeping was Mabel George, an editor at Oxford University Press. George was a passionate advocate of their work. She came from a family of printers and was knowledgeable about this aspect of publishing. She was determined to find printers who could do justice to the painterly approach of an artist such as Wildsmith. First published in 1962, Brian Wildsmith's *ABC* was ground-breaking; it won the Kate Greenaway Medal in Britain and the Carnegie Medal in the United States. Here, suddenly, was a book that overflowed with the textures, brush strokes, colours and sheer joy of paint. Wildsmith had been brought up among the grey stone of Yorkshire, but was trained at the Slade School of Fine Art. He has gone on to a lengthy and highly

Below: Gerald Rose's illustrations to *Old Winkle and the Seagulls* (text Elizabeth Rose; Faber, 1960) exemplified the emergence of a new sense of landscape and place in 1960s picturebooks. Gestural brush strokes evoke the breezy sea air.

One day, when all the other fishermen had given up hope, Old Winkle was still fishing beyond the sandbank, close to the Great Buoy. He knew that sooner or later fish were bound to come that way. While he sat there a scraggy old bird that he had fed many times alighted on the buoy. It stretched its neck and jerked its wings as it creaked and screamed. "Follow me!" it seemed to say, and Winkle, not at all surprised, started his engine.

Below: Brian Wildsmith's rich, painterly approach to picturebook illustration made new demands on rapidly developing printing processes in the 1960s. *Birds by Brian Wildsmith* (Oxford University Press, 1967) used the artist's name as part of the title, creating a gallery of paintings as much as a book.

Bottom: In this edition of Robert Louis Stevenson's *A Child's Garden of Verses* (Oxford University Press, 1966), Brian Wildsmith is given full rein to create dynamic page designs around each verse.

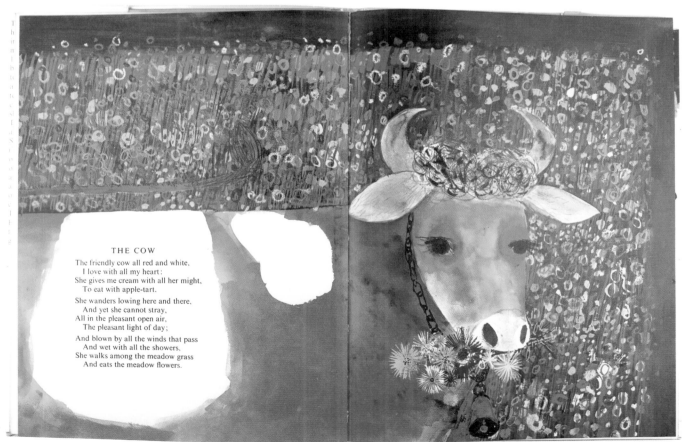

THE COW

The friendly cow all red and white,
    I love with all my heart:
She gives me cream with all her might,
    To eat with apple-tart.

She wanders lowing here and there,
    And yet she cannot stray,
All in the pleasant open air,
    The pleasant light of day;

And blown by all the winds that pass
    And wet with all the showers,
She walks among the meadow grass
    And eats the meadow flowers.

The railway did not run any more, but there were still six cottages in Railway Passage. The people who lived there were all rather old and rather poor.

The children who played on the rubbish dump, that was once a part of the old railway line, called them Aunties and Uncles.

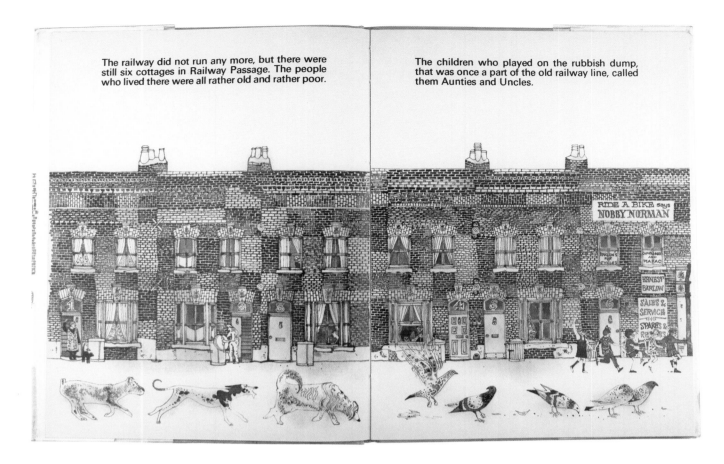

On the other side of the marsh was a dilapidated pier with an old painted barge moored alongside. This was the home of Ma Burley, retired now from a life on the river and canals,

her sole companions an old shaggy dog and two singing birds in a cage. Like most old people, they liked to tell the young folk of their travels and adventures in days passed.

successful career, combining book illustration and painting from his studio in the clear light of the south of France. His draughtsmanship and richly decorative compositions are especially appreciated in Japan, where the Brian Wildsmith Art Museum in Izukogen, south of Tokyo, was established in 1994.

Charles Keeping was, above all, a virtuoso draughtsman and printmaker whose instantly recognizable line is perhaps most familiar from his black-and-white illustrations to texts for older readers, such as the Carnegie Medal-winning *The God Beneath the Sea* by Leon Garfield and Edward Blishen (Longman, 1970). But in later life Keeping created a number of picturebooks that were highly original, personal and innovative. These often drew upon his working-class upbringing in the East End of London for their thematic content.

John Burningham's champion in the publishing world was Tom Maschler at Jonathan Cape, then an independent publishing company and now part of the Random House conglomerate. Burningham had studied at the Central School of Arts and Crafts

in London. In marked contrast to Wildsmith and Keeping, he was in no way a gifted draughtsman. His drawing could be described as clumsy and devoid of any trace of facility or mannerism. In his student days, his contemporaries laughed at his struggles in the life-drawing studio. But within a very short time of graduating he was forging a successful career in the graphic arts. Burningham's picturebooks are, as Deborah Orr observed '… clearly creative artefacts rather than commercial propositions, brought into being, above all, as an artist's expression of his own desire to create.'[2]

Burningham openly confesses to not being particularly interested in the idea of children's books. But through this medium, and perhaps partly because of his attitude, he communicates brilliantly, poetically and never patronizingly. *Borka: The Adventures of a Goose With No Feathers* was published in 1963 and won the Kate Greenaway Medal, an extraordinary achievement for a first book. Over subsequent years of continuous popularity, Burningham has continued to experiment and innovate, never

[2] *Independent*, 18 April 2009.

Opposite: Many of Charles Keeping's picturebooks evoke a strong sense of place, in particular the East End of London where he grew up. In *Railway Passage* (Oxford University Press, 1974) and his last book, *Adam and Paradise Island* (Oxford University Press, 1989), the setting is the lead character.

Below: John Burningham emerged in the 1960s as a major new talent. His richly evocative paintings demonstrate a keen interest in landscape, as in this spread from *Humbert* (Jonathan Cape, 1965). The sensual nocturnal cityscape is composed to draw the eye to the narrative focus – the horse in his stable.

Humbert felt terrible. He stayed awake all night thinking how unfair life was.

afraid to be challenging or ambiguous, as with the superb *Granpa* (Jonathan Cape, 1984) which we look at more closely in chapter 4. We draw attention to the serious side of Burningham because some of his most lasting books take up difficult issues, such as the illness and death of a beloved grandparent in *Granpa,* bullying and loneliness in *Aldo* and threats to the environment in hard-hitting picturebooks such as *Oi! Get Off Our Train* (Jonathan Cape, 1989).

Another profound influence on the development of the picturebook in the early 1960s was Ezra Jack Keats. Born in Brooklyn, New York, in 1916, Keats was an 'easel painter' who also worked as a commercial artist. His big breakthrough as a picturebook maker came with the Caldecott Award-winning *The Snowy Day* (The Viking Press, 1962). Keats' use of multicultural characters and urban settings was an innovation that transformed the children's picturebook landscape. His graphic techniques of merging collage and paint were also ahead of their time and highly influential.

The 1960s also saw the publication of *The Tiger Who Came to Tea*, one of those curious picturebooks whose enduring charm rather defies analysis. Its author, Judith Kerr, was a war refugee who escaped Nazi Germany to live in Britain. Her series of *Mog* books was equally successful, but the enigmatic, benign Tiger who arrives one day to quietly consume the contents of the fridge has a peculiar power that has kept him in print ever since the book was published in 1968. The writer Jenny Uglow has observed that: 'He somehow harks back to the fatal fascination of the charming, mysterious stranger, like the devil in ballads and fairytales who arrives without warning and disappears with equal suddenness, and who is longed for as well as held in awe.'[3] On a simpler, anecdotal level, many adults who grew up with this picturebook have described the excitement induced by the double-page spread that depicts the family setting off down the high street in the dark to find somewhere to eat, now that their home is emptied of food. A restaurant meal was a rare treat indeed for the 1960s British

[3] *Guardian*, 19 December 2009.

Left: Ezra Jack Keats brought a new perspective to the picturebook, breaking the stranglehold of all-white, middle-class characters and introducing an altogether more gritty, urban world, as in this spread from *Goggles!* (Macmillan, 1969).

Opposite: The enduring popularity of Judith Kerr's *The Tiger Who Came to Tea* is perhaps attributable to the lure of the 'mysterious stranger'. The illustrations reflect a 1960s vision of family life, yet there is a timelessness to the underlying concept.

So they went out in the dark, and all the street lamps were lit, and all the cars had their lights on, and they walked down the road to a café.

Sophie opened the door, and there was a big, furry, stripy tiger. The tiger said, "Excuse me, but I'm very hungry. Do you think I could have tea with you?" Sophie's mummy said, "Of course, come in."

So the tiger came into the kitchen and sat down at the table.

child. This is a book, though, in which very little happens and in which most of the rules of visual narrative are ignored.

The 'This is…' series by Miroslav Sasek began with *This is Paris* in 1958 and is laden with period graphic charm. The simple formula of playful visual tours of cities around the world has led to the books achieving classic status. Many of them have been reissued in recent times, though, sadly, too often not printed as well as they should have been.

Maurice Sendak may be the greatest illustrator for children of all time and was certainly one of the earliest to make an impact on educators and scholars, as well as on children, parents and the artistic community. *Where the Wild Things Are* (Harper & Row, 1963) was not Sendak's first picturebook, but it was the first one to make a huge impression on children and adults alike. Interestingly, it caused a furore when it was published, with many critics anxious that it would be too terrifying for children. As we write, it has just been made into a full-length feature film and is now part of the culture of childhood in the West. Many of the rules picturebooks had largely adhered to up to this point were broken as Sendak used every element of his artistry to powerfully convey his beguiling story. *Where the Wild Things Are* is essentially about love, but it also deals with anger, hate, obsessiveness, security, power relationships between adults and children, feeling out of control and the role of the imagination. Sendak tackles these issues through a simple story of impotent childish fury set against firm parental control (though we never see the mother). What makes it a masterpiece is the way he works on many levels to convey the depth of feeling of the young protagonist through colour, form and composition. Much of Sendak's huge output of picturebooks is equally challenging and brilliant, though nothing else has quite matched the affection that *Where the Wild Things Are* enjoys. He has also illustrated children's books by other writers superbly, perhaps most notably the *Little Bear* series by Else H. Minarik.

Below and opposite: Miroslav Sasek's *'This is…'* series introduced children to countries and cities around the world. What distinguished them from many such books was the artist's eye for the anecdotal detail of different cultures. *This is London* was published by MacMillan in 1959.

Tomi Ungerer is another influential artist who has spread himself across a range of artistic practices including the children's picturebook. In 2007 he opened the Musée Tomi Ungerer in his home town of Strasbourg, France. The museum houses his graphic works and collection of mechanical toys, as well as the works of other leading artists such as Ronald Searle and André François. First published in 1966, *Moon Man* is perhaps one of Ungerer's best-known picturebooks. The man in the moon watches from above and yearns to join in the fun on earth. When he finally manages to achieve his wish he is, of course, misunderstood and persecuted. But eventually he finds a way to get home, having satisfied his curiosity.

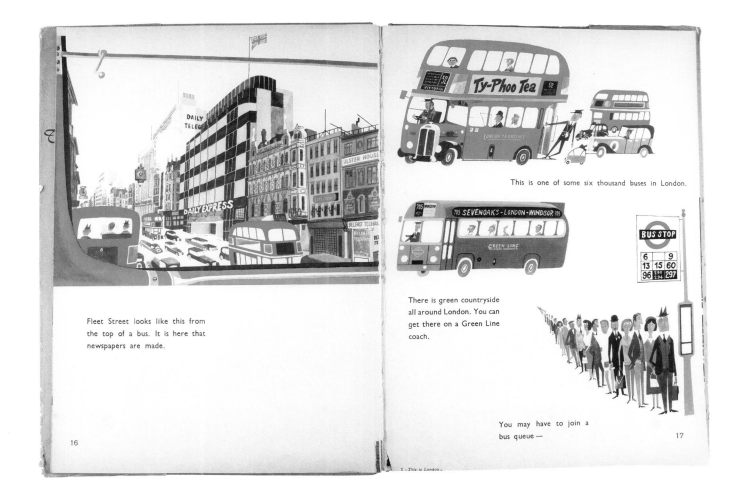

Fleet Street looks like this from the top of a bus. It is here that newspapers are made.

This is one of some six thousand buses in London.

There is green countryside all around London. You can get there on a Green Line coach.

You may have to join a bus queue —

16

17

Below: The genius of Maurice Sendak
has elevated picturebook art to a new
level. *Where the Wild Things Are* (Harper
& Row, 1963) deals poetically with the
subject of anger. The book has sold
around 20 million copies worldwide and
been translated into many other media,
including opera and film.

The 1970s onwards

Perhaps something of a forgotten genius, Roy Gerrard emerged as an author–illustrator in the late 1970s when he decided to abandon his job as an art teacher to give book illustration his full attention. Gerrard's combination of technical virtuosity in the medium of watercolour with a firmly tongue-in-cheek approach to epic historical subject matter gave birth to a highly innovative oeuvre that deserves to be remembered with the works of the best artists of his generation. Books such as *The Favershams* (Victor Gollancz, 1982) and *Jocasta Carr, Movie Star* (Farrar, 1992) demonstrate a distinctive and original approach to making picturebooks that delight children and amuse adults.

The books of Anthony Browne, Britain's Children's Laureate (2009–11), have been exciting children and teachers since the 1970s, when he first created picturebooks after an apprenticeship as a medical and greetings-card artist. His work is particularly acclaimed by academics, who applaud his inventive use of visual metaphor to create stories that are rich with significance, offering layers of meaning to be uncovered by old and young readers alike.

Most children, even quite young ones, find his work compelling and potent as well as funny and moving. Browne's meticulously rendered illustrations frequently carry subtle references to well-known paintings and often employ trompe-

Right: Roy Gerrard's strangely squat figures and exacting watercolour technique, combined with a surreal imagination, make him one of the most interesting picturebook artists to emerge in the 1970s. In this image from *The Favershams*, he condenses the ship to fit the format of the page and echo the shapes of the troll-like characters.

l'oeil effects and visual puns. *Gorilla* (Julia McRae, 1983), the earliest book to make a big impact, traces a little girl's yearning for real companionship with her father within a single-parent family (the mother is never mentioned). The child's isolation and desolation is beautifully depicted through haunting metaphorical imagery in subdued colours, all of which is contrasted with the bright happy fantasy life she leads on outings with the gorilla. In the following book, *Zoo* (Julia McRae, 1992), religious significance is afforded to another gorilla who, with immense dignity and sadness, is depicted within the shape of a cross (see p. 74). Here, Browne is clearly making a point about suffering and sacrifice. The rest of the book has many amusing features that make children laugh out loud, including the fact that people keep metamorphosing into animals. However, many of Browne's books carry challenging moral messages; in *Zoo* he continually draws the reader's attention to the links between animals and people, while highlighting captivity and freedom as a theme. This is never done in written text alone; the irony of badly behaved, thoughtless human beings visiting a zoo and exploiting the animals can be gleaned only from reading between the words and the pictures.

The prolific and versatile David McKee publishes regularly with Andersen Press. Well known for his amusing *Elmer the Elephant* and *Mr Benn* series for young children, he has also tackled strong themes such as war and injustice in his work (see pp. 127–28), and produced one of the earliest postmodern picturebooks for children: the incomprehensible but intriguing *I Hate My Teddy Bear* (Clarion, 1984). *Not Now, Bernard* (Andersen, 1980) is, perhaps, the picturebook that has made the most impact and is considered a contemporary classic by many people. Its clever interpretation of the adult tendency to patronize children and their imaginative minds brings delight to readers of all ages.

Janet Ahlberg enjoyed a rich creative partnership with her husband, writer Allan Ahlberg, until her untimely death aged only 50. Their collaborative work led to such masterpieces of ingenuity as *The Jolly Postman* (Heinemann, 1986), and its sequels, for which Janet won the Kate Greenaway Medal, and both partners received the Kurt Maschler Award in 1986. She had already won the Greenaway for the quieter classic *Each Peach Pear Plum* in 1978 (Kestrel). Janet's comic illustrations are not only outstanding as artwork, they also draw inventively on cultural aspects of life that provide challenge as well as delight for a young readership.

Below: The culture of picturebooks in China is growing. This unpublished page design illustrates the story of 'The Robe of One Hundred Kinds of Feathers' and is by the award-winning picturebook artist Cai Gao. Gao's work combines rich Chinese graphic tradition with more modern painterly techniques.

Picturebooks in the twenty-first century

In an increasingly global society it is reasonable to expect an increasingly global picturebook market. The arrival of the eBook should perhaps facilitate this internationalism further. In fact, it is not quite so simple. Although Disney has infiltrated most cultures, and many international publishing conglomerates produce intentionally global picturebooks, the picturebook as a cultural reflection of its place of origin seems to be obdurately enduring. At the same time as awareness of the picturebook as an art form is growing, many smaller countries and cultures are increasingly recognizing the importance of preserving their own languages and traditions. So, although the major names in the industry continue to be published internationally, happily there are still regional delicacies to be discovered. Many smaller nations provide subsidies to artists and publishers to ensure the continued production of indigenous picturebooks to be read alongside imported and translated works by international names. Less happily, few of these books seem to find their way into other languages.

Many new and emerging artists are represented in the chapters that follow. And the ones that are mentioned in this book are only a small selection from the vast number of important international and regional book artists who help to make up the current landscape of children's book illustration. The

Below: Jimmy Liao's *When the Moon Forgot*
(Little Brown, 2009)

emphasis here is on those who have been particularly influential as picturebook makers.

As well as creating his own books, the American Lane Smith has enjoyed a particularly successful collaboration with writer Jon Scieszka and designer Molly Leach since the dazzling debut of *The True Story of the Three Little Pigs* in 1989 (Viking). The hallmarks of this partnership include a witty, ironic relationship between word and image, inventive design, postmodernist features and technically dazzling artwork. The point of *The True Story of the Three Little Pigs* is not to believe a word written by the so-called author (Alexander T. Wolf) as everything he says is undermined by surrounding, counterpointing, images. Every new publication by Smith is more inventive than the last, and he has gradually moved from entirely traditional processes into digital media – a natural evolution for an artist who exploits the page with a cacophony of collaged textures and shapes.

Mini Grey is a highly inventive author–illustrator who has tried several other careers, including primary school teaching, theatre design and puppet making. She speaks of enjoying using her hands to make things as well as working with paint and collage on a flat surface, and her artwork has a certain theatricality. Her teaching experience means she knows her audience well and picturebooks like *Traction Man is Here* (Random House, 2005)

make absorbing fare for young children. They are also laced with postmodern irony and subtle references that keep the parent reader amused and entertained. In 2007 Grey won the Kate Greenaway Medal for *The Dish and the Spoon*.

Jimmy Liao's work has been phenomenally successful in his home country, Taiwan, as well as in many other Far Eastern countries, for a number of years, and he is now beginning to break into the English-language market. Liao worked in the advertising industry for 12 years before his first picturebooks, *A Fish With a Smile* and *Secrets in the Woods*, were published in the late 1990s. Much of his work has been translated into other media including film, theatre, animation and television. Liao's themes can be deeply spiritual, and frequently explore the experiences and emotions of everyday people in extraordinary situations.

Australian Shaun Tan's contribution to the evolution of the picturebook is immeasurable. This is not only because of the innovation, technical accomplishment and sheer creative ambition of his books, but also as a result of his writing and speaking on the subject. With books such as *The Red Tree* (Lothian, 2000) and the astonishing *The Arrival* (Lothian, 2007) Tan has taken the concept of pictorial text to a new level, exploring the ambiguity and potential for multiple meanings in visual sequence.

Below: In *The Arrival*, Shaun Tan explores the concept of displacement.

Below: The award-winning Japanese artist Katsumi Komagata's books transcend age groups and cultures by communicating primarily through the physicality of the book itself. In *Little Tree* (One Stroke/Les Trois Ourses, 2008), Komagata tells the story of the life cycle of a tree in minimal, highly poetic fashion.

German-born Jutta Bauer's picturebooks also deal with philosophical themes that are inclined to ponder the deeper meanings of everyday life. They are hugely successful in her native language but are only just beginning to penetrate other cultures through English translations such as *Grandpa's Angel* (Random House, 2005). Bauer's illustrations and writing have both simplicity and depth, and can convey narratives that are consequently multilayered.

When the Belgian artist and author Kitty Crowther received the Astrid Lindgren Memorial Award in 2010 it was recognition of her status as one of the world's leading pictorial storytellers. To receive such a prestigious award while still in her thirties was indeed an extraordinary achievement. Crowther is a master of the picturebook medium. Using a limited range of traditional media, predominantly pencil, coloured pencil and inks, she works in a direct, apparently spontaneous way that speaks intimately to the reader. As the jury for the Lindgren award stated: 'She maintains the tradition of the picturebook while transforming and renewing it… In Kitty Crowther's books, text and pictures form an integral whole.'

Maintaining, yet transforming and renewing, the traditions of the picturebook is an achievement to which only the very best contemporary picturebook makers can lay claim. In the following chapters we look at aspects of making and reading picturebooks from the perspectives of those who make, publish and read them.

Below: The cover of Kitty Crowther's *La Visite de Petite Mort*.

Below: Picturebook cultures are emerging rapidly from all corners of the world. *Obax* by André Neves has an African theme but is published in Brazil by Brinque-Book.

Ali morava a pequena Obax.

THE PICTURE BOOK MAKER'S ART

With the growing interest in picturebooks as a graphic form, some people ask: 'Is it art?' Equally, with more stylistic freedom creeping into the genre, others enquire: 'Is it suitable for children?' The answers to these questions vary greatly across different cultures but it is possible to argue that the picturebook has begun to fill a vacuum in narrative, representational graphic art. The suitability issue is discussed in chapter 5, but the fact that picturebooks are published primarily for consumption by children should not be a factor in assessing their artistic merit, and neither should the context of mass production. Context seems to have assumed a disproportionately powerful role in the world of art appreciation and can lead to a lazy approach to reading pictures. Even the father of the picturebook, Randolph Caldecott, suffered from such prejudice – in the *Pall Mall Gazette* (16 February 1886) he groaned that, 'artists say I am only a clever amateur'.

This chapter explores the unique art of the picturebook, from the perspectives of both its making and its meaning; and looks at the work of a number of individual artists from a range of cultural backgrounds, who describe their experiences and working methods. First, however, it may be useful to consider the idea of the picturebook as work of art and take a brief look at the kind of educational background from which the practitioner of this so-called hybrid art may emerge.

Opposite: Fabian Negrin's picturebook frieze to *Petit Robert et le Mystère du Frigidaire* (Notari Editions, Geneva, 2010). This publication brings together art, literature and music (accompanying CD by Aeschimann Simon).

Picturebooks as works of art

The very best picturebooks become timeless mini art galleries for the home – a coming together of concept, artwork, design and production that gives pleasure to, and stimulates the imagination of, both children and adults. Alternatively, mini theatrical productions may be a more appropriate analogy: it acknowledges the fusion of word and image that is key to the picturebook experience, while recognizing what Barbara Bader in *American Picture Books: From Noah's Ark to the Beast Within* (Macmillan, 1976) calls 'the drama of the turning page'.

The book as work of art is a concept that can be traced back centuries to the earliest handmade books. Today, the boundaries between the book arts, literature and 'commercial' graphic art can be seen to be merging in the children's picturebook. In *What Do You See? International Perspectives on Children's Book Illustration* (Cambridge Scholars Publishing, 2008) Magdalena Sikorska claims: 'It is probably only a slight exaggeration to say that many contemporary picturebooks are the last bastions of visual culture in the medieval sense of coded messages.'

In 2007, OPLA, the archive of artists' books for children, was created at Merano City Library in Italy, reflecting and celebrating the area where art (whatever we mean by that) and the picturebook converge. Here, the work of artists who have pushed the boundaries of the book as an artefact can be enjoyed by scholars and children alike. As Maurizio Corraini writes in the catalogue of the tenth anniversary exhibition:

Handled works!!! An explosive possibility which means they can be touched and owned, a chance to come into direct contact with art. This is a way to begin good habits, especially among children, which leads them to consider art as something that directly affects them and not, as often happens, a distant world that they can visit only occasionally.[1]

Corraini is explaining that all of us, not only children, benefit by having this opportunity to hold and feel what are essentially works of art. Where a unique personal artistic vision combines successfully with an ability to make contact with minds and hearts from the world of childhood, magic can follow. This mysterious 'remote landscape' of childhood is one that, in the words of Ilaria Tontardini, '… we adults perceive as belonging to some distant part of ourselves'.[2]

[1] Maurizio Corraini, *Children's Corner*, 2007.
[2] Quoted in the catalogue to the 'Metaphors of Childhood' exhibition. Editrice Compositori, 2009.

Education and training

As discussed in the previous chapter, the artistic giants of the genre have established themselves in the consciousness of many generations of children and adults. Maurice Sendak, Eric Carle, Bruno Munari, Kvêta Pacovská and John Burningham, to name just a few, have made a lasting impression on the art of the picturebook as well as on an audience of millions. How have these and other artists emerged? Can their skills be taught? The latter is a question that goes to the heart of the nature of art and design education. There are many undergraduate and graduate/postgraduate courses in general illustration, and an increasing number in some form of narrative illustration. But there is little consistency in the kind of education the great illustrators received even as recently as during the twentieth century. Quentin Blake, for example, studied English at Cambridge University, and Edward Ardizzone attended evening classes in figure drawing, where he was taught by the artist Bernard Meninsky, while serving his apprenticeship as a clerk in a City of London company. There is also considerable diversity in the

Below: Edward Ardizzone was one of the most popular and influential British illustrators of the twentieth century. But his formal art education was limited to evening classes in life drawing. He made many prints and drawings of the experience.

Below: Hippopotamus from *One Five Many* by Květa Pacovská.

backgrounds of the newer generation. Some have had little formal art education, while others have had a more classical training in fine art or graphic design.

'Drawing is another way of thinking,' said the influential British graphic artist Edward Bawden.[3] It is an assertion that hints at why art and design has not been considered an academic subject until relatively recently, and the difficulties it has experienced in being absorbed into contemporary university culture. Traditionally, art schools have been places where aspiring artists have come to learn skills from masters; in other words, art and design has always been taught by artists and designers. In the applied arts, this has been seen as being especially important, with most teaching delivered by professional practitioners who give a small proportion of their time to teaching, both as a supplement to their incomes and as a way of 'giving something back' – and, indeed, gaining inspiration from contact with students. Many of the artists featured in this book have taught illustration in art schools as visiting lecturers. Over the years,

many illustrators have managed to combine high-profile careers in publishing with parallel roles in education. Examples include Quentin Blake at the Royal College of Art in London, William Stobbs at Maidstone College of Art and Steve Guarnaccia at Parsons in New York City.

In Edward Bawden's time as a student at Cambridge School of Art in the 1920s there would have been little in the way of a curriculum, let alone multiple assessment criteria and learning outcomes. His days were spent drawing from classical casts and meticulously rendering letterforms – thinking through drawing. Through most of the twentieth century, art schools were autonomous institutions that existed outside the university system, and were managed and taught by artists and designers rather than academics. The recent absorption of these schools into universities has resulted in an as yet unresolved culture clash, where the world of learning through making, of thinking through drawing, crashes headlong into the world of lecture-based learning, predefined learning outcomes and quantifiable

[3] William Feaver, 'Drawing his own conclusions'. *Observer Magazine*, 8 March 1987, p. 32.

Left: William Stobbs was one of a number of artists who combined productive careers as illustrators with full-time employment in art schools.

Below: *Off to Windmill Hill*, an ink-and-wash sketch by Edward Bawden. Bawden studied at Cambridge School of Art and the Royal College of Art in the 1920s, when students spent much of their time drawing from classical casts and learning calligraphy.

knowledge. Amazingly, it is more than 50 years since the American artist and illustrator Ben Shahn foretold and examined these clashes in his treatise, *The Shape of Content* (Harvard University Press, 1957). In it he pondered the awkward relationship between creative expression and the academy:

…there is always the possibility that art may be utterly stifled within the university atmosphere, that the creative impulse may be wholly obliterated by the pre-eminence of criticism and scholarship. Nor is there perfect unanimity on the part of the university itself as to whether the presence of artists will be salutary within its community, or whether indeed art itself is a good solid intellectual pursuit and therefore a proper university study.

The conflict is particularly apparent at the level of doctoral research where the PhD, the highest academic degree, is traditionally awarded for research that begins with a research question and ends with proven research findings – a hitherto alien concept for the creative or expressive artist, for whom research can have an entirely different meaning. The picturebook has, however, been the subject of a growing body of academic research in recent years, some of which is touched on in chapters 3 and 4. An increasing number of artists are now undertaking research at PhD level through personal creative practice, advancing knowledge through thoughtful making. This is important: it builds on existing research from the 'outside', and reveals new knowledge about the process and practice of making picturebooks, to add to what is already known about a completed artefact and the ways in which it can be read. Such creative practice-led research in the arts is still in its infancy and is the subject of much, often heated, debate. The relationship between theory and creative practice is at the heart of this debate, and is a key concern of this book in the context of the making and meaning of children's picturebooks.

Above: For many art students in the twentieth century, the classical cast played a key role in developing an understanding of form.

Left: Ben Shahn's influential book is as relevant today as when it was published in 1957. Like Edward Bawden, Shahn's work happily straddled the fine and applied arts; both artists believed the same personal standards should be set whether working for oneself or a client.

The picturebook artist

So the question remains: How does the picturebook artist emerge? Can the art of the picturebook be taught? Fortunately, artists are far too unpredictable to allow for easy answers to these questions, but there are many skills – conceptual, creative and technical – that can be acquired with the right sort of help. There are also unique individual gifts and talents that can be damaged by the wrong kind of teaching. The mid-twentieth-century British painter and illustrator John Nash recalled his illustrious older brother Paul dissuading him from undertaking a formal training: '… he used to tell me how lucky I was to begin free from the disadvantages of conventional training.'[4] Paul Nash was extremely protective of what he saw as his brother's 'innocent eye'.

Although most art-school lecturers engaged in teaching illustration would agree that drawing is the fundamental skill of the illustrator, it is hard to find any consensus on what it actually means. Some perceive it primarily as a formal skill, an ability to convincingly render three-dimensional form on a two-dimensional surface. Others think in terms of intuitive, gestural

[4] Sir John Rothenstein, *John Nash*. MacDonald & Co, 1983.

For most illustrators, the sketchbook is where their individual visual language emerges and evolves, away from the scrutiny of others; student sketchbooks, Cambridge School of Art. **Left, top**: Ballet class drawings by Merja Palin; **bottom**: Carnaby Street collage by Karen Thompson. **Overleaf, top and bottom**: Sketchbook pages by Antoaneta Ouzonova; **middle**: Sketchbook pages by Katrin Lang.

mark-making. More usefully, we might consider *why* we draw rather than *how* we draw. The American graphic artist Saul Steinberg defined drawing as 'a way of reasoning on paper'. Everyone will draw differently, see differently and think differently, but the apparently simple act of trying to articulate an idea or experience visually on paper, and in sequence, is still the basis for most illustrators' work.

It is the particular individual sense of purpose behind the image-making process that dictates and shapes the evolution of a visual identity in an artist's work rather than any conscious pursuit of style. Nevertheless, generations of children have grown up learning to recognize instantly the work of individual picturebook artists through each one's personal visual 'signature'. For the aspiring artist, it is tempting to borrow stylistic idioms from these familiar 'auteurs'. It can seem an easy option to imitate a particular quality of line that may appear effortless. But a genuine pictorial voice emerges through a lengthy personal dialogue with the real world. Usually, this process happens in the sketchbook, free from any consciousness of an audience or its age. Initially, this is all about learning to see. Through drawing we come to realize that we don't know things we thought we knew through cursory visual contact. Keith Micklewright expresses the chicken and egg conundrum eloquently in *Drawing: Mastering the Language of Visual Expression* (Laurence King Publishing, 2005):

Without being able to 'see' it is difficult to draw, but without being able to draw it is a problem learning to see... an initial and more formidable phenomenon is how often people need persuading that the ability to recognize objects is not really seeing.

The art of the picturebook maker therefore involves thinking in, and communicating through, both pictures and words. It is an art that is cultivated through a process of the interdependent skills of seeing and drawing.

Learning to see

The term 'visual literacy' was first coined by John Debes in the 1960s. Although there is no unanimously agreed definition of its meaning, this hasn't inhibited its increasing use. As Clive Phillpot pointed out in *Visual Literature Criticism: A New Collection* (Southern Illinois University Press, 1979), verbal language seems to fail us badly in this area:

The familiar words 'literacy' and 'numeracy' have more recently been joined by the word oracy, but when it comes to describing the skill of seeing (as opposed to looking) we seem to be stuck with the phrase 'visual literacy', which suggests rather the skill of reading a pictorial image. One can, of course, see the reasons for the coupling of these two words, but the absence of such words as 'visuacy' or 'picturacy', or some similar verbal idiocy, still seems significant. The phrase 'visual literacy' attests to the dominance of visual culture by the verbal.

It is fair to say that artists and academics will have different ideas on what it means to see. As early as 1969 Rudolf Arnheim lamented, in *Visual Thinking* (University of California Press, 1979), the tendency of the education system to relegate the role of the plastic arts to one of therapy:

Today, the prejudicial discrimination between perception and thinking is still with us. We shall find it in examples from philosophy and psychology. Our entire educational system continues to be based on the study of words and numbers. In kindergarten, to be sure, our youngsters learn by seeing and handling handsome shapes, and invent their own shapes on paper and in clay by thinking through perceiving. But with the first grade of elementary school the senses begin to lose educational status. More and more the arts are considered as a training in agreeable skills, as entertainment and mental release.

What these extracts seem to be saying is that, although we are constantly reminded we live in an increasingly visual culture, it may be that there is still a tendency to regard thinking and drawing as very separate activities.

Thinking through drawing

Drawing is not, or shouldn't be, a passive activity. As we draw from observation, the marks we make do not only describe the form or contours of the subject, but they also begin to express those aspects of it that we are, consciously or unconsciously, most interested in or curious about as individuals. This is how the individual, personal language of picture-making begins to evolve. The American illustrator James McMullan sums this up nicely when writing about his experience of teaching a group of illustration students at the School of Visual Arts in New York, and trying to help them find a natural sense of identity in their work:

I didn't want to teach them a style of drawing. I wanted to teach them a way of thinking for themselves through drawing... (Ironically, I seem to have succeeded in helping students understand their own work when I encouraged them to think about their subjects rather than themselves.)[5]

Many artists have spoken of the lifelong search for the 'innocent eye' in their work. In other words, they are expressing a desire to unlearn, to cast off skills and mannerisms and learn to see the world through the eyes of a child. Such a common yearning reveals the subtle relationship between artistic vision and the means by which we articulate it – how facility or skill can begin to feel as if it is getting in the way of pure expression. Micklewright, on the other hand, argues that skills should not be seen as a hindrance:

Spontaneity should not be confused with innocence, and knowledge should not be seen as corrupting, but liberating. Nobody would tell an author that learning to read and write would compromise the imagination or advise a musician to cherish incompetence.

A slightly tenuous analogy perhaps but, as the author points out, it is pointless to aspire to the kind of genuine *naiveté* of artists such as Alfred Wallis or Henri 'Le Douanier' Rousseau, who are the exceptions that prove the rule.

[5] Heller and Arisman, *The Education of an Illustrator*. Allworth Press, 2000.

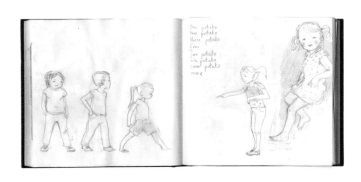

The sketchbook plays a key role, therefore, in the education of the illustrator, providing a private world of exploration of things, people, ideas, places and occasional shopping lists. This precedes all other, more applied approaches to picturebook-making, the ones that can be taught in a more tangible way, such as visual, sequential pace and word–image relationships. Within this private world of the sketchbook the need to get things down for future or present reference, to capture things and ideas before they escape, can gradually help to overcome self-consciousness and aid the process of establishing a personal voice. Those artists who combine a personal draughtsmanship with a strong sense of something to say are the ones who are most likely to enjoy a lengthy career in picturebook-making. An ability to apply one's work to a range of moods and subject matter is also a great advantage. Switching from the playful to the lyrical or poetic as seamlessly as John Burningham, Quentin Blake or Alexis Deacon do is a tough call.

Below: These pages from Alexis Deacon's sketchbooks demonstrate the kind of intense visual and intellectual curiosity that underpins his work as a picturebook maker.

Visual communication

The term 'visual communication' is commonly used to describe the general subject area of graphic design and illustration. And it is the concept of communication that some see as the dividing line between the fine and the commercial or graphic arts. In *The Education of an Illustrator* (Allworth Press, 2000), the illustrator and educator Marshall Arisman quotes the sculptor David Smith as defining commercial art as 'art that meets the minds and needs of other people' while fine art is 'art that meets the mind and needs of the artist'. Of course, we like to put things in boxes in this way but the boundaries between areas of the arts are inevitably blurred, and Arisman rightly points out that, by Smith's definitions, many illustrators are fine artists and many fine artists are illustrators. While there are many artists working in the domain of the picturebook whose works are highly authorial, personal, often poetic statements, it may be argued that the ability to communicate visually is paramount. At the same time, the layers of messages and meanings conveyed may be increasingly open to subjective personal interpretation in the modern picturebook, in the same way as they are in artworks, which are more likely to be experienced in the context of the gallery.

The rest of this chapter examines the picturebook maker's art through conversations with a number of artists and student artists, touching on issues of visual research, sequential planning, editorial input and the cultural differences and expectations that can impact on the success and/or publishability of a picturebook.

Student case study: Capturing a sense of place

Andrew Gordon
Last Summer by the Seaside

The outcomes for *Last Summer by the Seaside* were submitted for Andrew Gordon's final masters project at Cambridge School of Art. Although this particular project was not subsequently published, it played a major role in the artist being given a contract to illustrate another picturebook text. Gordon's work during his masters studies had always incorporated observational drawing and a great deal of sketchbook research. He was keenly interested in the traditions of British art that are rooted in landscape and a sense of place, embodied by artists such as Edward Bawden and John Lawrence. Initially, he had little idea of what to focus on in this project, but it was agreed that he would begin with an open-ended period of visual research in his native north-east England. It was also agreed that the final form of the project should be allowed to grow out of this process:

Initially the North Yorkshire setting came into it when I was researching the idea for a non-fiction book about Captain Cook. I was interested in the setting and atmosphere – fishing cottages perched on cliffs, boats tied in the harbour, fishermen at work, the cold North Yorkshire weather. With the initial sketchbook work I was exploring various subjects and themes about the seaside. It was an opportunity to explore the

Below and opposite: Andrew Gordon's picturebook project grew out of an immersion in 'place'. Beginning with sketchbook work on location, he went on to develop rudimentary storyboards and eventually a finished pictorial narrative.

possibilities of media, composition and subject matter, to be playful without having to produce images for a specific text.

He filled sketchbooks with a mixture of location drawings, character sketches and unstructured flights of fancy, all the while experimenting with different media. Much of the subject matter focused on the small coastal towns and resorts of the area. As the final deadline for the project neared, Gordon became increasingly anxious about how exactly he would use this material. But previous projects had perhaps arrived at 'outcome' a little too quickly. Various ideas were floated for narratives that would take place against the backdrop and mood that had been established in the sketchbooks. But these were feeling a little contrived and incongruous. Gradually it was the sense of place that asserted itself as the main character of this project, and a picturebook began to emerge in the form of a young child's winter recollection of a day at the seaside.

I remember the storyboarding stage being quite a struggle, but it was through the process of note-making and drawing that I arrived at the idea of the boy's reminiscence. I remembered visiting these places for days out as a child and thought I could combine these memories with the observational work. This idea seemed the most honest way to develop the body of work I had produced so far into a children's picturebook. From there, I drew up a very rough storyboard showing the basic framework for the story and the concept for each spread. I avoided roughing out the spreads in too much detail in order to retain spontaneity when working on the finished illustrations. Delaying the writing of the actual text enabled me to accommodate changes to the sequence as I went along, and allowed me time to consider what the text was going to be – which I found very beneficial as I did not feel confident about writing it at the beginning of the project.

Sitting by his rainswept urban window he recalled the sights, sounds, smells and tastes of a long, hot summer day by the sea. It had become clear (as it often does) that this would not be a case of writing a story and then setting about illustrating it. The pictures would carry the main essence of what was to be conveyed. The text would gently augment them, spoken entirely as dialogue by the child narrating his thoughts and memories. The result is a picturebook project that powerfully projects an intimate, nostalgic sense of place.

Finally all that remains is a faint whistling of the cold wind and the distant rolling of the sea as the sun starts to set. Downstairs I hear Mum calling my name.

Overhead giant seagulls squawk.   I watch them wheel and glide in the sky.

Student case study: Narrative non-fiction

Madalena Moniz
Manu is Feeling… From A to Z

Madalena Moniz is from Portugal. She was in the first semester of her final year as an undergraduate student of illustration at the University of the West of England in Bristol when she completed *Manu is Feeling…From A to Z*. Her images resonate with the subtlety of her ideas and have a quiet lyrical intensity that rewards slow contemplation. The delicate, fragile linework seems to give each image a powerful emotional presence. This is an alphabet book with a difference. Avoiding traditionally playful approaches to this kind of picturebook, Moniz has sought out more complex relationships between word and image on each spread. The adjectives chosen to represent each letter are descriptive of a state of being – emotional or physical – and are often described through visual metaphor, requiring the reader to make links across several steps between word and image.

Through its design and conceptual consistency the book has a strong visual identity, using white space to emphasize scale and tension. The developmental sketchbook work evidences a fastidious process of thinking through drawing.

Below and opposite: Madalena Moniz uses sketchbooks to methodically try out various possibilities for her alphabet book. Patterns, letterforms and characters are explored in detail to test their graphic potential.

From a publishing perspective, this book might be seen to break too many rules for some markets, where age categories are rigidly adhered to. Most alphabet books are, of course, designed for very young readers. Placing, as it does, greater demands on the visual literacy of the reader, *Manu is Feeling…* may find its natural home in cultures where picturebooks are allowed to appeal across wider age ranges.

Moniz was clear that she wanted to tackle a picturebook at this stage of her studies. She says:

I chose to do an alphabet book because I liked the idea of focusing only on the image and spread compositions – not on a story, and the challenge that presented in holding the viewer's interest without a story to follow. The first step was choosing a theme – a thread that would run through the whole thing and make the viewer want to turn the page. It couldn't just be 'A for Apple' and 'B for Ball'. It had to have a deeper meaning so the viewer wouldn't lose interest along the way.

So I thought about feelings. To illustrate something that can't be seen, such as feelings, requires creativity, which is the main reason why I liked the subject. I chose to use only one character for the whole book. All the feelings from A to Z would be this boy's feelings, hence the title 'Manu is Feeling…'.

For my characters to be really convincing I usually base them on real people. For this one I used old photographs of my brother, and I named him Manu after my brother Manuel. He would wear the same clothes throughout the book, except on a couple of letters to relate to a different weather or activity. I used strong colours on his clothes and a light brown for his hair.

Moniz was keen to avoid the obvious representations of emotions such as 'S is for Sad'. Rather, she wanted the whole image to project the particular emotion, making the viewer think about it and explore the relationship between the image and the word. The structure of the book would be consistent throughout: the letter and word would be on the left page of

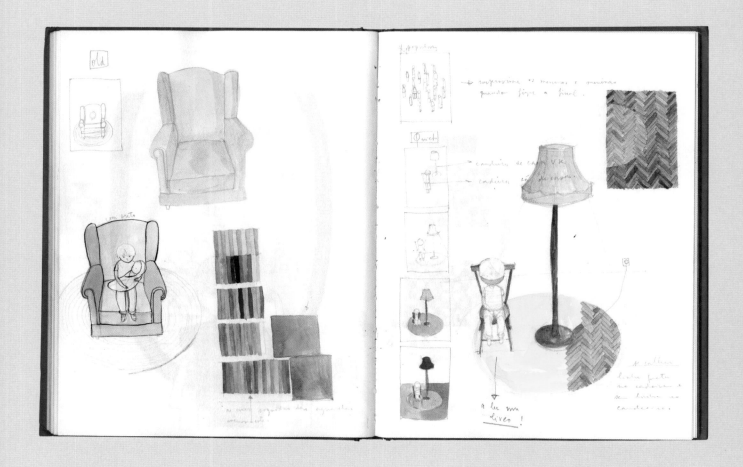

Gigantic

Love

the spread and the image representing the feeling would always be on the facing page. She felt confident about this simple approach from the outset. Pattern plays an important part in the design and communication of mood:

The letter would be inserted in a pattern or a pattern would be inserted in the letter, always a pattern that would relate to the feeling or the image in question. I like to use patterns on my work. I researched and created patterns in order to find the appropriate one for the different images and used them to help convey the feeling. During the making of the book I would think of words and images together, rather than thinking of a word and then trying to illustrate it. Sometimes the image would come first and then I'd need to search for the perfect word. Sometimes it was the other way round. My ideas didn't come in any organized way! They would come at any time so the trick is always to get them down in the sketchbook as quickly as possible. There is a great deal to work out when making a picturebook and much of this can only be realized during the actual process of making.

Throughout this process Moniz kept a sketchbook in which all the development work and studies evolved. Referring to these notes and sketches, she developed each of the final spreads, in no particular order, except that she began with the ones she was most excited about. Using A3 (11.69 × 16.54 in) watercolour paper she worked up the final designs with ink and a very fine brush for the linework, along with watercolour washes: 'I tend to give a delicate look to my images with thin lines, soft colours, the use of pattern and the small scale of the figures.' Many spreads were worked and reworked until Moniz was entirely happy with the outcome. All the artwork was handmade, with Photoshop used to clean up the background and fix small mistakes: 'This is how I like to use Photoshop – just as a final tool. I like the look and feel of handmade artwork.'

Opposite and below: Finished spreads for *Manu is Feeling...From A to Z.*

Melancholic

Professional case study: The innocent eye

Beatrice Alemagna
Un Lion à Paris

Beatrice Alemagna is one of the most admired artists in children's picturebooks today. She has won many international awards and prizes. As well as working in the field of children's literature, she has worked as a poster artist for the Centre Pompidou in Paris for over ten years, and has designed fabrics and ceramics. Her graphic work combines a rare depth of visual literacy with a gentle, poetic humanity and a fearless approach to experimenting with media and materials.

Originally from Bologna in Italy, Alemagna is now based in Paris. She is perhaps an example of the kind of artist whose language is untaught or unteachable in the sense that it seems to come so directly from the heart, in the form of a visual poetry apparently untainted by conscious technique or facility. Her educational background is interesting in this respect. Growing up in a cultured environment, she absorbed the books of Bruno Munari, Emanuele Luzzati, Leo Lionni and Tomi Ungerer among others. She read the fables of Gianni Rodari, Italo Calvino and the Brothers Grimm. Alemagna says that she has known she wanted to do what she now does since she was eight years old: 'As a child, illustrated books were my private space, for me alone. I would leaf through them for hours, sniffing the smell of the paper. They made me dream.'

In adolescence she studied literature. Although all she wanted to do was draw, her family encouraged her to take a

Below and opposite: A few of Beatrice Alemagna's early studies for *Un Lion à Paris*. At this stage the drawings are simple compositional studies and the character of the lion is only just beginning to emerge.

broader cultural education before attending art school. Eventually Alemagna accepted a place at the Instituto Superiore per le Industrie Artistiche (Superior Institute of Industrial Arts) in Urbino. Here she found that the focus was on design, typography and editorial graphics with little attention to drawing. At the time she found this very hard. The school has since developed illustration as a subject specialism. In the summers she was able to attend short courses in illustration, notably under the tutelage of Stephan Zavrel and Kvêta Pacovská.

This lack of direct tuition in illustration during the main period of study once again begs the question whether there are instances where a nascent, personal visual language is best protected from some elements of a traditional, formal art education. Certainly, it is possible to argue that Alemagna's graphic work manages to retain that element of *naiveté* that is so powerful when combined with sophisticated design skills. Here, a thorough grounding in typography and graphic design seems to have provided a perfect structure in which to place a highly sensitive and expressive visual language. Speaking about this, Alemagna says:

Yes, I felt that I suffered a lot through not studying the techniques of drawing, not knowing how to use acrylics or watercolours and so on. But in the end I realized that I like to invent my own techniques, to improvise with oils or pastels, experimenting with tissue paper or wool. I do think that studying graphics gave me a sense of composition, of weight and space. In terms of my drawing, perhaps it has retained a 'purity', that's to say a closeness to my childhood. It isn't 'formatted' behind a precise style or technique. This is something that I have only recently learned to value.

I know that I have a multitude of personalities that express themselves differently in my drawing. Perhaps if I had learned or acquired a particular technique I would have settled into a particular way of working and would not have fallen into this perpetual 'search'. It's a painful process but one which is intimate and personal. This is why I don't know how to illustrate texts that don't touch me personally and also why my books don't tend to resemble one another. I look back at each book as representing and reflecting a stage of my personal evolution.

Un Lion à Paris (Autrement Jeunesse, 2006) was awarded a special mention in the 2007 Bologna Ragazzi Awards. Published in large-format hardback, unusually bound on the long side, it tells of a lion's arrival in Paris and his surprise at not being feared, noticed even. He tours the city in his melancholy state as an outsider, searching for something, and ultimately returns to his place on a plinth in the square. This exquisitely

beautiful, poetic book is appropriately described as follows by Anna Castagnoli: 'Beatrice Alemagna doesn't just draw, she composes symphonies with the colours of music.'[6]

Alemagna says of the original inspiration for the book:

The idea for the story was born in a conversation with a friend who lives near the statue of the lion at Place Denfert-Rochereau, and who spoke to me about how much the Parisians love this lion. I had already found inspiration in this lion, so proud in the middle of the square. I had been to look at him many times and the idea grew to use him as a way of telling the story of 'the stranger', looking and feeling different in an unknown city. I also wanted to create a character with charm in his attitude to others. The theme of identity, in its different facets, is a central one in most of my books. In making the images, I wanted to recreate the Paris that inspired me through the films of Truffaut and Goddard and through the photographs of Henri Cartier-Bresson among others.

It's the story of a visitor with his shifting view of the city and the reality that surrounds him. In fact, the book is in many ways autobiographical. Each scene that the lion encounters in Paris is one that has importance for me. The Café de Flore where I would go after my meetings with a publisher, Beaubourg because of my work in creating the posters, and Montmartre where I would meet a very dear friend who is the lady in the book with the white hair. L'Isle St Louis was near to where I lived in my early days in Paris and the Canal Saint-Martin is where I later came to live. The baguette under the arm is a motif that has always had great resonance for me. There are also tiny portraits of my father, my sister and I. So when I am asked whether the little girl on the last page is me, I reply, 'Absolutely not. I am the lion!'

Graphically, in this book I feel that there is a use of space that is different in comparison to all my other books. I wanted to show real places in Paris but reinterpreted in my own way, showing the city as it is, but also as I see it. It is an ode of love, of my love of Paris – a ballad to the streets. I didn't want to make an 'infantilized' city, all jolly houses and pointy roofs. I have tried to show the real city, with its chaos, its grey buildings. I've just added my view. I wonder whether, in its realization, 'Lion' is really a book for children, because it speaks to the child through the eyes of an adult, albeit an adult with perhaps a childlike eye.

Above all, I wanted to create images full of detail, full of people but retaining a regard for composition and space, not overcrowding each page. I do storyboard my books but my working method is a little bizarre. If I decide on the final form of the book too soon, I lose the emotion and joy. I usually prefer

to just have an idea in my head, remaining a little fluid and allowing it to flow on to the paper without knowing exactly what will happen. Sometimes I tear up dozens of sheets of paper before arriving at the right image. It's not the most economical way of working!

Such a delicate process requires a real relationship of trust between the artist and publisher. Alemagna's work in many ways exemplifies the very different attitudes to visual aesthetics in mainland Europe compared to those in English-speaking countries. Her books are enormously successful in several European countries and also in East Asia, especially South Korea, but she has only just begun to break into the English-language market. This may be because Britain's longer tradition of illustration for children, with its roots in representational painting, has led to narrower perceptions of graphic 'suitability' in picturebooks.

---

[6] www.lefiguredeilibri.com/?p=69

Below and opposite: Preliminary sketch and finished artwork for *Un Lion à Paris*.

Below: Cover of Ajubel's *Robinson Crusoe*.

Professional case study: A wordless book

Ajubel
Robinson Crusoe: A Wordless Book

Now based in Valencia, Spain, the artist Ajubel is originally from Cuba. His visual work covers a wide range within the graphic arts, but he is perhaps best known for his posters and for his editorial illustrations in leading newspapers and magazines. Ajubel's entirely pictorial version of *Robinson Crusoe* evolved through discussion with Vicente Ferrer, at the Valencia-based publishing house Media Vaca (see pp. 178–79). *Robinson Crusoe: A Wordless Book* was awarded the Ragazzi Award for fiction at the 2009 Bologna Children's Book Fair.

Vicente and Ajubel had known each other for some time. The distinctive books from this small, independent publishing house are normally produced in limited (usually two) colours, always with the greatest attention paid to design and production. Media Vaca books also come with the reminder on the back covers, *LIBROS PARA NIÑOS… NO SÓLO para niños!* (BOOKS FOR CHILDREN… NOT JUST FOR Children!). Vicente explains that he had been thinking about producing a book in full colour for some time and that Daniel Defoe's famous story had always been one of his favourite texts. He says:

I wanted to make a book with Ajubel, and with his background – growing up on an island, and his sense of colour, he seemed the perfect choice for this project. I decided to get rid of the

Below: Finished artwork for Ajubel's *Robinson Crusoe*.

verbal text altogether as I didn't want to abridge it in any way. The narrative is simple and highly visual. I like the way that in this novel it is clear that nature is not always your friend. Often, in Robert Louis Stevenson for example, the tropical island is portrayed as a romantic paradise. Ajubel's images are full of subtle narrative detail. He wanted to make a book suitable for all ages so he was careful to avoid violence.

A close working relationship between publisher and artist/author is essential to the success and integrity of a book. But this relationship will vary greatly depending on the size and nature of the publisher. At large conglomerate publishing houses many people are involved in the editorial, design and marketing elements. This can lead to a well-rounded book that serves its market well or it can have a reductive, flattening 'design by committee' effect on the artistic ambition of the book. In the case of *Robinson Crusoe: A Wordless Book*, the editorial process was collaborative and relaxed. Ajubel describes it as follows:

The idea for the book came from Vicente at Media Vaca. I was given total freedom from the beginning including deadline, colour, creativity, number of pages. I only had to respect the format of the series and not use words. Our conversations about the progress of the book generally took place over lunch, and were relaxed and entertaining. Obviously the storyboard changed during the creative process, a few changes were suggested during our conversations and other intuitive changes took place along the way to produce the book that we see now.

Ajubel tends to work initially through drawing on paper and then developing colour on screen. However, he finds that the processes of drawing and 'painting' digitally tend to merge and become one:

… nowadays drawing and colour for me are almost the same. I have been working with the computer and the electronic pen for many years and almost don't make the distinction any more. At the end of the day these are just tools.

Whether we can label *Robinson Crusoe: A Wordless Book* a picturebook, in the sense of our previously offered definitions, is unclear. Like all Media Vaca books, it happily rejects the rules, breaking out of the 32-page picturebook stereotype and pretty much every other convention. It tells the story entirely through full-bleed double-page spreads, without the use of comic-strip framing conventions. Ajubel's paintings have an almost visceral sense of the primitive, propelling the narrative forward with a strong left to right dynamic, and an acute awareness of the page-turning impulse. The visual text is highly stylized, but at the same time articulate in its communication of the narrative.

Below: Finished artwork for Ajubel's *Robinson Crusoe.*

THE PICTURE BOOK AND THE CHILD

… the picture book, which appears to be the cosiest and most gentle of genres, actually produces the greatest social and aesthetic tensions in the whole field of children's literature.[1]

Sheila Egoff

Preamble

I am in a library in the middle of a primary school, with a few six-year-olds, some of whom can't yet read print. On a large table, I've laid out varied picturebooks which the children can select at will. Two boys are sharing Anthony Browne's *Zoo* roaring with laughter, fingers pointing at favourite illustrations, trying to compete with each other in finding more hilariously funny examples of humans metamorphosing into animals.

One little girl is gazing sadly at the final spread of John Burningham's *Granpa* which suggests, but does not say, that the grandfather has died. Another is deeply absorbed in Jan Pienkowski's *Haunted House*, carefully opening every flap of every pop-up. She is 'reading' the book on her own after we have already looked at it together three times in a row. The intensity of her gaze and the seriousness of her scrutiny teaches me that some children need several 'lookings' to get a proper sense of a picturebook. I'm impressed by the strength of the children's desire to make meaning of these texts, and the pleasure they take in them is infectious. I've explored most of these books with the children several times and now they are enjoying them independently for the fourth, fifth, maybe the tenth time. Some older children walk by on their way to the gym. Noticing me and the picturebooks they stop to take a look, giving groans of delight and longing – as if they were in a wonderful toyshop at Christmas. What is it about outstanding picturebooks that provokes such reactions in children? They appear to weave themselves seamlessly into the lives of young readers, encouraging a perpetual readiness for the unexpected, and a welcome for both experienced and inexperienced readers alike.

Morag Styles

[1] Sheila Egoff, *Thursday's Child: Trends and Patterns in Contemporary Children's Literature*, p. 248. American Library Association, 1981.

We hadn't got a map of the zoo so we just wandered round. Me and my brother wanted to see the gorillas and monkeys, but we had to see all these boring animals first. We went into the elephant house which was really smelly. The elephant just stood in a corner stuffing its face.

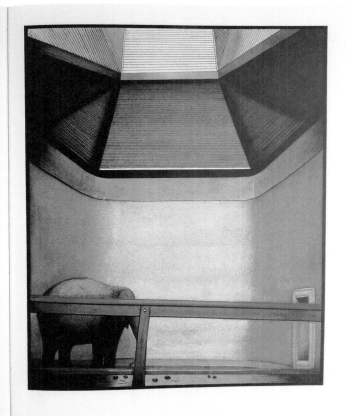

Children reading picturebooks

The nature of picturebooks is discussed earlier in this volume, but it is useful to consider the definition by the American academic Barbara Bader, which is the one most favoured by scholars of children's literature. In *American Picture Books: From Noah's Ark to the Beast Within* (Macmillan, 1976) she writes:

A picture book is text, illustrations, total design; an item of manufacture and a commercial product; a social, cultural, historical document: and foremost an experience for a child. As an art form it hinges on the interdependence of pictures and words, on the simultaneous display of two facing pages, and on the drama of the turning page.

As Bader points out, picturebooks are simultaneously art objects and the primary literature of early childhood, offering compelling drama for readers through the interaction of the visual and verbal narratives. It can be hard work to make sense of the 'readerly gap' created by the space and tension between what the words say and what the pictures show, and young readers only make the effort if the picturebook is worth the trouble. Fortunately, there are many excellent examples that repay readers' endeavours. Most of the texts by the illustrators highlighted in this book come into this category.

In the definition above, Bader infers that picturebooks are a means by which we integrate children into a culture, yet the best of these books also encourage divergent readings as we will show. In historical terms, different periods construct childhood differently and this is represented in the literature produced for the young. For example, in the so-called golden age of children's literature (in the 1920s and 1930s between the two world wars), there was a desire to emphasize the beauty and innocence of childhood. Just think of Ernest Shepard's illustrations for A.A. Milne's poetry and his Winnie the Pooh stories – they delighted readers then and are still popular today. We may be living in a so-called postmodern age where playfulness, rule-breaking, fragmentation and uncertainty are commonplace (and feature in many challenging picturebooks), but romantic and idealized representations of childhood still appeal to adult nostalgia, and are still represented in many picturebooks.

The picturebooks we highlight in this volume are not these cosy ones, but those that are more risk-taking in every sense – demanding themes, sophisticated artistic styles, complex ideas and the implied notion of a reader as someone who will relish these challenges and take them in their stride, as long as the books are engaging. As Maurice Sendak put it:

Children… will tolerate ambiguities, peculiarities, and things illogical; will take them into their unconscious and deal with them as best they can… The artist has to be a little bit bewildering and a little bit disorderly…[2]

Some authors create complicated 'metafictive' picturebooks that playfully draw attention to the fabric and materiality of the book itself and are full of mischievous subversion of the normal conventions. Lane Smith and Jon Scieszka's *The Stinky Cheese Man* (Viking, 1992), for example, highlights, makes fun of, and turns upside down – sometimes literally – every unspoken rule of the picturebook. A character from the book (Little Red Hen) argues with publishers' conventions on the back cover; parts of the dedication page are upside down and amusing asides are directed at the reader; the contents page is a carefully

Opposite: Anthony Browne's books, such as *Zoo* (Julia MacRae, 1992), have fascinated children and academics alike for their use of visual metaphor to explore a range of themes.

[2] Maurice Sendak, *Caldecott & Co: Notes on Books and Pictures*. Viking Penguin, 1989.

crafted jumble of jokes, incomplete sentences, 'The End' and so on.

Sendak is also a master of such effects. *We are all in the Dumps with Jack and Guy* (HarperCollins, 1993) has no title or author on the front cover. Instead, there is a stage set that introduces some of the themes Sendak is playing with. As well as the familiar stylized urchins from some of his other books (such references are called intra-textual), which are reminiscent of Charles Dickens' young vagabonds, there are skinny children with bald heads, suggesting chemotherapy treatment or concentration camps or the victims of AIDS. The written text includes 'Kid elected President' and 'Meaner times, leaner times'. The reference to homelessness is further picked up in the endpapers, which are blank, brown cardboard-type paper suggestive of basic cardboard shelters.

The sheer rule-breaking potential of a couple of pages from *The Stinky Cheese Man* and *We are all in the Dumps…* gives some insight into the challenges offered by picturebooks today – and, incidentally, the respect the authors have for their young audience by assuming they will work hard to tease out meaning and find the book rewarding. Such picturebooks require advanced skills on the part of the young reader, who has to negotiate meaning, reading between the lines and the pictures.

Below: The term 'metafictive' has been employed by academics to describe the self-referential play evident in books such as *The Stinky Cheese Man*. Children are assumed to have a full grasp of postmodern irony when negotiating the works of Jon Scieszka and Lane Smith. In this title page the designer, Molly Leach, makes an important contribution to the meaning of the pages.

This book is
dedicated to our
close, personal,
special friend:
(your name here)
—J.S. & L.S.

I know. I know.
The page is upside down.
I meant to do that.
Who ever looks at that
dedication stuff anyhow?
If you really want to read
it—you can always stand
on your head.

INTRODUCTION

A long time ago, people used to tell magical stories of wonder and enchantment. Those stories were called Fairy Tales.
Those stories are not in this book. The stories in this book are almost Fairy Tales. But not quite.
The stories in this book are Fairly Stupid Tales.
I mean, what else would you call a story like "Goldilocks and the Three Elephants"? This girl walking through the woods smells Peanut Porridge cooking. She decides to break into the Elephants' house, eat the porridge, sit in the chairs, and sleep in the beds. But when she gets in the house she can't climb up on Baby Elephant's chair because it's too big. She can't climb up on Mama Elephant's chair because it's much too big. And she can't climb up on Papa Elephant's chair because it's much much too big. So she goes home. The End.
And if you don't think that's fairly stupid, you should read "Little Red Running Shorts" or maybe "The Stinky Cheese Man."
In fact, you should definitely go read the stories now, because the rest of this introduction just kind of goes on and on and doesn't really say anything. I stuck it on to the end here so it would fill up the page and make it look like I really knew what I was talking about. So stop now. I mean it. Quit reading. Turn the page. If you read this last sentence, it won't tell you anything.

JACK
Up the Hill
Fairy Tale Forest
1992

SURGEON GENERAL'S WARNING: It has been determined that these tales are fairly stupid and probably dangerous to your health.

Defining visual literacy

'Visual literacy' (see p. 56) is a contentious term as there are so many different ways of conceptualizing what it means to read image, let alone 'multimodal' texts that contain a mixture of verbal and visual elements. Kate Raney, who in 1998 wrote her doctoral thesis on visual literacy, puts an emphasis on social practices associated with cultural and ideological considerations that seem to fall somewhere within the disciplines of art, education and philosophy. Her definition is simple and persuasive. Visual literacy is:

… the history of thinking about what images and objects mean, how they are put together, how we respond to or interpret them, how they might function as modes of thought, and how they are seated within the societies that gave rise to them…[3]

Our view is that in this increasingly visual world it is essential that children learn the skills of looking, appreciating and interpreting visual material, including its design. This is something most children do quite naturally at an early age as they are drawn to pictures, colour and form, but this instinct can be developed and enhanced by enlightened teaching and by learning how to analyse visual texts insightfully. From a very early age most children draw unselfconsciously, merging the seen and the imagined. Learning to look and see through drawing promotes and nurtures vital visual literacy skills. Sadly, the activity of drawing is often undervalued in primary education. Furthermore, once children have mastered print it is important that they continue to extend their awareness of the visual so that they are able to value, understand and intelligently analyse visual material from advertisements and computer games to fine art, film and animation. Picturebooks seamlessly provide lessons in looking at, and evaluating, visual texts.

[3] Kate Raney, 'Visual Literacy: Issues and Debates'. Middlesex University School of Education, 1998.

Visual texts and educational development

Before discussing some of the critics who are best known for writing about children's interpretations of picturebooks (other theoretical approaches to the genre are discussed in chapter 4), it is necessary to consider briefly how the way children develop is linked to visual literacy. It is generally assumed that they follow a fairly predictable developmental pattern in most things, including their understanding of visual codes.

Jean Piaget, one of the earliest and most influential educational psychologists, argued that children can make sense of the world only within the limits of their developmental stage. Writing from the 1930s until well into the second half of the twentieth century,[4] Piaget broke new ground in his attempts to describe how children's minds develop. One of his great insights focused on the role of maturation in children's increasing capacity to understand the world around them. While his theories of how children learn were innovative in their day, they are now considered too narrow and rigid to take account of the huge variations in child development. For example, Piaget wrote that between the ages of two and seven (what he called the pre-operational stage) children are so egocentric in their thinking that they are unable to consider any viewpoint different to their own. He believed that between seven and eleven years (the concrete operational stage) children develop the ability to undertake many formal operations, but that it is only after twelve that they are capable of abstract thought. Since then, several distinguished psychologists, most notably Lev Vygotsky and Jerome Bruner,[5] have argued that Piaget's theory is too simplistic, and pointed out that some children can achieve abstract thought before the age of eleven, or sympathize with

Below: Children seem to identify strongly with the way pictures can often express feelings and fears more clearly than words, as in Satoshi Kitamura's *Lily Takes a Walk*.

the views of others before they are seven. With specific reference to visual literacy, these ideas are important because it is often the pictures in picturebooks that enable children to interpret ideas in a more sophisticated way than might be expected given their age. What most educators and psychologists do agree about is the huge potential of learning by looking.

In the research project by Evelyn Arizpe and Morag Styles discussed below, there was ample evidence that some young children were able to formulate clever and perceptive responses to picturebooks, far beyond what might be expected of them developmentally. The converse was also true, in that some older children made interpretations that were rather more inadequate than would be expected for their age group.

Arizpe and Styles conducted their research between 1999 and 2001, on the detailed reactions of 100 children to the picturebooks *Zoo* (Julia McRae, 1992) and *The Tunnel* (Julia McRae, 1989) by Anthony Browne, and *Lily Takes a Walk* (Corgi, 1987) by Satoshi Kitamura; and discovered how discerning even a very young and a bilingual readership can be. There was illuminating evidence of children drawing in response to the picturebooks: what they couldn't always express in words they could often show in their visual work. Since the publication of this research in *Children Reading Pictures* (Routledge, 2003), other researchers have, as a matter of course, videoed interviews and drawing sessions with children, so that their physical responses (body language, gestures, etc.) can be taken into account, and tabs can be kept on how they draw, which can be very revealing.

Kate Noble, who contributed to the project, went on to investigate, for her doctoral thesis, how 24 children responded to picturebook versions of *The Frog Prince* (including editions by Jan Ormerod, Walker Books, 2002; and Jon Scieszka and Steve Johnson, Viking, 1991). She focused particularly on their drawing processes, their own artwork and their physical reactions to the picturebooks, and also used conventional interviews and semistructured discussions. She shows how when children draw and talk about picturebooks they reveal their cognitive, aesthetic and emotional awareness and, indeed, contribute to our understanding of the development of visual literacy. Some of Noble's findings are discussed in Janet Evans' recent book, *Talking Beyond the Page* (Routledge, 2009).

In *Literacies Across Media* (Routledge, 2002), Margaret Mackey highlights the two-way interaction between the human body and the text in the act of reading. She describes it as a physical as well as cognitive activity – a playful process of negotiation, imagination, orchestration, interpretation and experimentation, using visual strategies of noticing, searching, exploring, hypothesizing, comparing, labelling and strategizing. Anything but passive! She also explores these ideas in *Art, Narrative and Childhood* (Trentham, 2003) in a chapter on children's responses to David Macaulay's *Shortcut* (Houghton Mifflin, 1995), which one ten-year-old describes tellingly as 'the most thinking book'.

---

[4] See, for example, Jean Piaget, *The Child's Construction of Reality*. Routledge, 1955.
[5] Two excellent volumes that summarize these arguments and explore developmental learning are Margaret Donaldson's *Children's Minds* (Fontana, 1984) and David Wood's *How Children Think and Learn* (Blackwell Publishing, 1998).

Soon, she comes to the last corner. This is the best moment of all. She can see the light in her window and smell her supper cooking.

How children respond to picturebooks

You can learn on a stained-glass window and then when it comes to a book you're ready and you can look at the pictures and know what's happening.
Tamsin (aged 8)

Tamsin was one of the children who took part in Arizpe's and Styles' research project, and she already knows not only that you take images as seriously as words in picturebooks, but also that you have to learn how to read them insightfully. This is something she picked up looking at the pictures in stained-glass windows when she went to church as a little girl. Barbara Bader has suggested that the foremost function of the picturebook is as 'an experience for a child'. In the sections that follow, we show some of the research evidence of how children experience picturebooks.

Of course, we can never know all the subtle effects picturebooks have on children because a child doesn't have the language skills to convey them and, indeed, some aspects of a visual experience cannot be conveyed verbally. And the younger the child, the harder it is for them to express the nature of their response. In the research that led to *Children Reading Pictures*, in addition to answering interview questions the children were given the opportunity to look at the same book several times and each session ended with a free-rolling discussion among those of the same age group. The further invitation to the children to draw in response to the picturebooks (with no time limit) offered a chance to get as close as possible to their understanding of the texts, which they often could not articulate. Frequently, more was learnt from the drawings and open-ended discussions than from the formal interviews.

The 100 children in the sample were aged four to eleven, and represented fluent readers, children who had just started to read independently and those who were struggling with print. Their real names are not given in any part of this chapter but the quotations are verbatim. What comes across strongly is the children's sheer excitement and pleasure, and their willingness to engage with the challenges picturebooks offer. As Kathy (aged 6) put it: 'A good story's got to have a problem and the problem's in the pictures.' Kathy is probably also referring to the fact that the text in many picturebooks is straightforward enough, but the 'complications' are presented in the pictures (see 'Counterpoint and duet', pp. 94–96).

Responding to word–image interaction

There is a sort of love affair between very young readers and their picturebooks, especially before they can read print. Amy (aged 5) said: 'I always remember pictures. I sometimes forget words.'

Older children can discriminate between the different functions of words and pictures. Below are some of the replies children in the project gave to the following questions:

- Do you find the words or the pictures more interesting?
- Do they tell the same story in different ways?
- Would the words still be good without the pictures?
- Would the pictures still be good without the words?

*… if it was just writing you wouldn't really feel like you were in there because there was nothing to show you what it was really like. OK, you could use your imagination, but **if you want to know what the girl's point of view is you'd have to have pictures to see**.*
Tamsin (aged 8) (our emphasis)

*Some books are better without the pictures because then you can make up your own thing, but I think this is better with pictures... **the words need the pictures more than the pictures need the words.***
Keith (aged 10) (our emphasis)

Well I couldn't really choose between words and pictures because the illustrations are excellent and the words he uses just capture your imagination and then if he didn't have any pictures you could still understand because the words he uses describes it very well.
Gemma (aged 9)

*The writing doesn't explain everything what you think about... **So I like the pictures better because then you can think more stuff.***
Lara (aged 10) (our emphasis)

... the pictures seem to bring out the story.
Sue (aged 11)

Analysing colour for significance

Children are appreciative of illustrators and often try to work out how they achieve their effects and what these effects signify. Young readers are especially sensitive to colour and tone, and seem to analyse its significance quite naturally. Note the serious attention children pay to every aspect of pictures that intrigue them. Here's Seamus connecting darkness with fear in *Lily Takes a Walk*, followed by three children who make careful judgements based on colour analogy.

Erm, it's getting dark, so I think [Nicky's] a bit worried so he's going to look around and make sure nothing tries to snatch him or anything. See, because at the beginning it's broad daylight and she's out for the whole day. If you turn the pages it gets darker and darker and darker... I like the way he's done the colours, and made them really blue and swirly colours and it's a bit black.
Seamus (aged 7)

Cause the way the shade's done on that, it's lighter then it gets darker, cause the sun is on part of the roof, it makes this part dark and this part light and how... it's not just like flat. I think it's really wonderful the way they've done the shadow...
Tamsin (aged 8)

M (aged 10): She probably feels sorry for the animals.
I [Interviewer]: So how do the colours signal that?
M: Cos she's wearing that black and dark... dull and dark colours.
I: Right. So you wear black for funerals. And what do black and purple represent?
M: Sad and sorryness.

I like how he's mixed them colours up. Like there's light green, then a little darker then really dark and then lighter again. He's mixed all the colours up together to make them look like they're from the sunlight as it's shining on the curtains and you can see the shadows as well...
Louise (aged 6)

Unfortunately, there is no space to show children drawing in response to picturebooks, but there is plenty of evidence to reveal how their imaginations were fired by what they 'read'.

Here's Polly (aged 5) talking to herself as she draws.
I'll just switch my brain on... that's the house in the distance that's why it's really small... Now here I am going to use another green. Isn't grass two different shades of green? This is a lime shade of green...

Reading body language

Even the youngest children are good at reading body language, something they probably learn from cartoons on television. Some ten-year-olds responded sympathetically to the emotive image of an orangutan crouching miserably in a corner in *Zoo*.

I [Interviewer]: How do you think the orangutan is feeling?
E (aged 7): Very sad.
I: What makes you say that?
E: Well, if he's not showing his face then it might be because he's sad and he just doesn't feel like it... he hasn't got anything around him. Like the elephant, no natural habitat.
S (aged 10): He is sort of similar to a human, he should be treated like a human.
L (aged 11): Because he looks like he's got hair coming down... really long hair.
T (aged 11): And it has got grey hairs like an old person.
S: He looks like he's got his hair in a bun at the top and like...

Reading visual metaphors

While children enjoy a good story, most look for more than that in a picturebook. So it is not surprising that, when faced with complex multimodal texts, they puzzle over what the pictures might symbolize or how words and images together construct meaning. Without knowing the vocabulary, or understanding terms such as visual metaphor, they nonetheless interpret visual symbols, sometimes with extraordinary aplomb. In the first example below, a five-year-old understands the symbolic significance of the fact that, in the final endpaper of *The Tunnel*, the ball (which represents the older brother) and the book (which represents his sister) are positioned together, representing a new harmony between the fighting siblings.

I [Interviewer]: Why do you think the ball and the book are together on the final page?
S (aged 5): Because now the ball and the book can cuddle.

Matt (aged 8) knows that the piece of piping on the ground between the brother and sister in *The Tunnel* refers to the hostility between them. Ruth (aged 8) shows emotional literacy by recognizing the close bond between the siblings in the story, even though they fight a lot:

You can see the brother don't want her near, because you can see the pole and he don't want his sister to cross it. Like me and my sister. We don't actually get along very much, because we fight a lot. Well when she's upset, I really, well I don't feel good.

Looking and thinking

After reading *Zoo,* many of the children commented that it made them think. Browne's theme of captivity and freedom emphasizes the relationship between human beings and animals, often to the detriment of the former, but this is never mentioned in the written text. It has to be inferred from the illustrations and through the ironic juxtaposition of word and image. As Sue (aged 10) remarked: 'The people are acting like animals or what we think animals act like.'

He doesn't just want to say the animals want to be free – blah, blah, blah. He leaves you to find it out a bit better… **makes you keep thinking about things***.*
Erin (aged 7) (our emphasis)

The most powerful image in *Zoo* is a gorilla with a soulful, intelligent gaze who is depicted in four rectangles that make up the shape of a cross. As Yu (aged 4) put it: 'He's got like… a grandpa's eyes.' None of the children recognized the religious iconography in their first few readings of the book but all of them, even the four- and five-year-olds, saw it eventually. This demonstrates the value of rereading picturebooks. Indeed, both authors of this book believe you have to examine a complex picturebook at least half a dozen times before you begin to make inroads into its possibilities.

The final spread of *Zoo* features the young narrator looking thoughtful for the first time in the book. Browne depicts him silhouetted against the bars of a cage on the verso page, making an ambiguous connection between human beings and captivity. On the recto the architect-designed zoo buildings are set against a beautiful but perhaps threatening purple/blue

night sky with two wild geese flying into the unknown. Dan (aged 7) gave an emotional response:

D: *He's in a cage and been sad and all that lot. On the little picture there is hardly any [border] but then on the big pictures [of animals] there is a big black outline round the pictures… on this page it hasn't got a border at all, so it looks like he's an animal and he's also free.*
I [Interviewer]: *Do you think the boy was feeling bad about the visit to the zoo?*
D: *Yeah, and sometimes when your worst dreams, you like cry in the middle of the night and all that lot… I like this page because it's all black, dark and all that lot. And then birds come along and fly away. And it's nice and peaceful in the dark…*

Rising to the challenges offered by picturebooks

We have tried to show the purposeful way children approach picturebooks. They love to be amused, but they also want to be challenged. We have seen children sit for more than an hour with a picturebook in single-minded pursuit of its essence. The best illustrators are those who respect their young readers and never sell them short.

Opposite: Children seem to understand the use of visual metaphor in Anthony Browne's *The Tunnel* quite easily.

Below: Lauren Child's *Who's Afraid of the Big Bad Book?* gives children a riot of word–image fusion and the occasional *mise en abyme* on which to muse.

Just then the telephone started to ring.

Sticking telephones in fairy tales had seemed funny at the time, but Herb could see that they could turn out to be rather a nuisance.

Below: Children read Steve Johnson's
illustrations to Jon Scieszka's *The Frog
Prince Continued* in various ways, but
the visual clues augment the general
feeling of ennui.

E (aged 7): *I really love his books (Browne).*
I [Interviewer]: *I want to know why you say that.*
E: *Well he doesn't just say, 'I'll just write a story'… he actually thinks about it. Or he plans it ahead and then he does really good pictures and the pictures tell a different story, the same story only in a different way.*
P (aged 7): *I look carefully and I see what may be the problem because you see the dog notices things and the girl isn't noticing, so then I split the book into half and I see what Lily's seeing and… I will look at the dog and see what he's doing.*
I: *So you get sort of one side and then the other side?*
P: *And try and put them together.*

When you are little things scare you more than when you're bigger… When you are little sometimes your imagination just wanders and then when you are older you can tell things look like that or not…
Angus (aged 9)

The rest of this chapter looks at evidence from other research projects connected with the authors of children interacting with picturebooks.

Looking and learning

Picturebooks engage minds as well as hearts, and make cognitive demands on the reader. The most challenging books make children think in new ways which they often find deeply absorbing. In the examples that follow, provided by Louiza Mallouri, then a student on the Cambridge Faculty of Education masters course on children's literature, young readers of *Who's Afraid of the Big Bad Book?* (Lauren Child, Hodder, 2003) speculate about the picture within a picture where the central character, Herb, holds a copy of the book with himself on the cover.

E (aged 7): *That's quite funny because he's on a book and he is in a book and he is in a book (pointing to the picture of Herb in the book on the cover). And so he is in a book and it goes on forever… cos he's reading the book we are reading.*

D (aged 8): *It's funny because we are reading it now and he's reading it there except in this book, Herb is in it and when he is reading it right now he is not in it…*

Children today grow up in a highly visual world, and quickly overtake their parents in their ability to master new multimodal technologies. In most cases, they encounter moving images as early as, if not earlier than, books and easily learn how to interpret visual codes. For example, when children see drooping flowers in cartoons they soon realize this means that things are not good for the protagonists. Here two five-year-olds discuss with Kate Noble (in her unpublished doctoral study) the opening spread of *The Frog Prince Continued* (Puffin, 1994) where the prince and princess both look thoroughly miserable.

I [Interviewer]: *The flowers are unhappy!*
Kate: *How do you know the flowers are unhappy?*
T: *Because they're drooping.*
K: *Why are the flowers drooping?*
T: *Because they haven't any water.*
I: *And no sunlight.*
T: *They have got sunlight. It is light in there [points].*
K: *But not enough.*
I: *Yeah, that's what I mean. Not enough.*
K: *OK. Why do you think the artist has put the flowers drooping?*
I: *Because he thought that cos they were unhappy they'd forgotten about the flowers.*

Affective responses to picturebooks

Children sometimes make strong emotional bonds with the authors of the books they love. This lively piece of transcript discussion provides evidence of a group of children aged seven and eight acting out, as well as reacting with delight, to *Who's Afraid of the Big Bad Book?*[6]

L [Louiza]: *Who is that?*
C: *Herb.*
D: *No! No! It's Goldilocks!*
[All laughing]
D: [pretending to be Herb trapped in Goldilocks' body] *Oh my goodness, look at my hair!*
[All laughing]
L: *What is she doing here?*
C: *She's writing. She's writing.*
D: *I can't stand my hair, please send a hairdresser!*
[All laughing]
C: *She's writing because she wants to be the best star. The divinely…*
E: *I love Lauren Child!* [takes the book and kisses it]
[All laughing]
D: *If pictures are real and people can jump out of books…*
E: *Yeah, that would be so cool! And they will come alive… And then imagine it happen… Imagine!*

---

[6] A longer extract from Louiza Mallouri's M.Phil essay can be found in *Postmodern Picturebooks*. Sipe & Pantaleo, 2008.

Conclusion

Mention has already been made about the picturebook's key function as the first literature most children experience, usually in the guise of a narrative that combines word and image. Jean-Paul Sartre, the existentialist French philosopher, once said 'childhood decides everything', and it is important that a wide range of challenging, inventively illustrated picturebooks features strongly in children's early reading diet. But we have also shown that picturebooks are for all ages, and there are plenty of excellent examples to tempt, excite and challenge readers of eight years and above. The picturebook is also the main vehicle through which children are introduced to art, so parents and teachers will want to ensure they are given examples by the finest illustrators. This chapter has demonstrated how reading picturebooks can encourage children to think deeply. It has also shown how picturebooks can provide a safe space in which children can explore emotional relationships, including some of the big issues of life – love, divorce, death, violence, bullying, environmental issues and so on. There is no topic so taboo or taxing that it has not been tackled in a picturebook. We need to value this extraordinary visual literature that gives so much pleasure to children, yet makes demands on, and contributes so positively to, their cognitive, emotional, aesthetic and intellectual development. After all, as Perry Nodelman put it in *Words about Pictures* (University of Georgia Press, 1990), good picturebooks 'offer us what all good art offers us: greater consciousness – the opportunity… to be more human.'

WORD AND IMAGE, WORD AS IMAGE

Below: In *Come Away from the Water, Shirley*, John Burningham creates a structure for two worlds. The prosaic comments of the parents on one side of each spread are offset by full-bleed visual representations of the child's vivid imagination on the facing page.

Mind you don't get any of that filthy tar on your nice new shoes

In most contexts, illustration provides a visual accompaniment to words, a prompt or aid to the imagination that aims to augment the overall experience of a book. But in the case of picturebooks, words and pictures combine to deliver the overall meaning of the book; neither of them necessarily makes much sense on its own but they work in unison. And the most satisfying picturebooks create a dynamic relationship between words and pictures. Often this duality can be in the form of a playful dance, where images and words can appear to flirt with and contradict each other. Increasingly, the boundaries between word and image are being challenged, as the words themselves become pictorial elements and the outcome as a whole is 'visual text'. In the last few decades, the potential for creative exploration of this relationship has been recognized and exploited by picturebook makers in increasingly sophisticated ways, and is also appreciated by a rising number of critics and theorists interested in complex picturebooks.

As scholars, artists and children alike have discovered, the nature of the relationship between word and image clearly lies at the heart of what makes a picturebook good, bad or indifferent. Fabulous artwork can be admired, but if the words don't interact with the pictures in interesting ways the book as a whole will

not be a success. On the other hand, the written text may be superb but if the pictures are bland the overall effect will be mediocre. The very best illustrators – Maurice Sendak is a good example – create memorable picturebooks where the words and pictures connect brilliantly. A few very talented picturebook writers, such as Martin Waddell, Jon Scieszka and Chris Raschka (an illustrator who, like an increasing number of artists, also writes stories for others to illustrate) have collaborated with illustrators to produce picturebooks that deliver a satisfying interplay between the two forms of visual text.

Theorizing picturebooks

Academic theorists analyse aspects of picturebooks and visual literacy from a range of perspectives. Their studies over the last 30 years have looked at and recognized not only the dynamic relationship between word and image in children's picturebooks, but also the importance of visual design and the multiplicity of meanings offered by the genre. Below is a brief survey of some of the approaches of influential scholars in the field.

Perry Nodelman and Margaret Meek wrote seminal books that have changed our understanding of how picturebooks achieve their effects: *Words About Pictures* (University of Georgia Press, 1990) and *How Texts Teach What Readers Learn* (Thimble Press, 1988) respectively. Nodelman argued that placing words and pictures 'into relationship with each other inevitably changes the meaning of both', so that they are 'more than just a sum of their parts'. He believed it was the 'unique rhythm of pictures and words working together that distinguishes picturebooks from all other forms of both visual and verbal art'. He also claimed that 'words can make pictures into rich narrative resources – but only because they communicate so differently from pictures that they change the meaning of pictures. For the same reason, also, pictures can change the narrative thrust of words.'

As the title of her book makes clear, Meek's focus was about the way that quality picturebooks subtly teach children the rules of narrative; in particular, she pointed out that a picturebook is 'an icon to be contemplated, narrated, explicated by the viewer… the story happenings are in the pictures which form the polysemic text'. Since then many artists and scholars have tried to describe the interaction between words and pictures in different ways using various metaphors. Allan Ahlberg talks of 'interweaving' for the word and image relationship: 'You can come out of the words and into the pictures and you get this nice kind of antiphonal fugue effect'[1] while Meek herself uses 'interanimate' to suggest the dynamic way words and images work together.

In *Looking at Pictures in Picture Books* (Thimble Press, 1993), Jane Doonan's focus is on the aesthetic, as she analyses form, line and artists' particular styles of illustration. She points out that 'every mark displayed in a picture is a carrier of meaning, beginning with the chosen material or medium and how the mark is made'. Her insightful analysis of pictures in picturebooks draws on both a deep understanding of the artistic process and knowledge of young learners, in her case secondary school pupils. She also makes the important point that, 'Once a child discovers how much there is to be made from looking into pictures, reading a picturebook becomes wonderfully taxing' – something the previous chapter attempted to exemplify.

One of the earliest influential articles on picturebook codes was by William Moebius who in 1986 drew readers' attention to elements of design and expression, including colour, perspective, position, size, frame and line. Later, in *Reading Images: The Grammar of Visual Design* (Routledge, 1996), Gunther Kress and Theo Van Leeuwen applied a detailed semiotic analysis to picturebooks, showing that there is a 'grammar' to visual design. One simple example is that the verso side of most picturebook spreads deals with the known whereas the recto favours new information, thereby encouraging the reader to turn the page. Nodelman also emphasizes the importance of semiotic analysis: 'Making ourselves and our children more conscious of the semiotics of the picturebooks through which we show them their world and themselves will allow us to give them the power to negotiate their own subjectivities…'[2] David Lewis provides a useful summary of Nodelman's and Kress and Van Leeuwen's approaches in *Reading Contemporary Picturebooks* (Routledge, 2001). In this volume, he also makes some reference to how children respond to visual texts, as well as showing the complexity of this art form and different ways of examining it.

Both Sylvia Pantaleo (University of Victoria) and Lawrence Sipe (University of Pennsylvania) have considered the potential of sophisticated picturebooks in numerous individual books and articles which often also take account of the responses of young readers. *Postmodern Picturebooks: Play, Parody, and Self-Referentiality* (Routledge, 2008) which they edited together, offers examples of some of the foremost international scholars, themselves included, who are working in this exciting genre. In this volume, Margaret Mackey, the renowned and prolific Canadian scholar of visual texts, demonstrates how exciting postmodern picturebooks – such as those by Chris Van Allsburg, Sara Fanelli, Emily Gravett, Peter Sis, Lane Smith, Colin Thompson and David Wiesner – 'interrogate the static qualities of the picturebook' demanding a 'multi-constructed reading stance' and 'help to create a plasticity of mind that is also honed on other textual forms'. Here Mackey is referring to the fact that picturebooks have to compete in a market that brims with sophisticated high-tech films and games. She believes that 'when other dynamic texts are so seductively available, knowing that books can also play lively and entertaining postmodern games is a lesson that cannot be learned too young'.

---

[1] Quoted in David Lewis, *Reading Contemporary Picturebooks*. Routledge, 2001.
[2] Perry Nodelman, 'Illustration and Picturebooks' in Peter Hunt, *International Companion Encyclopedia of Children's Literature*. Routledge, 2004.

Word and image interplay

After this brief look at some of the key theories surrounding word and image interplay, it is time to examine some outstanding picturebooks, starting with several examples that are artfully simple and satisfying. The work of two further important critics, Maria Nikolajeva and Carole Scott, is discussed in this context.

Filling in the gaps

In *How Picturebooks Work* (Routledge, 2000) Nikolajeva and Scott use the term 'complementary' for picturebooks where the images reflect and expand what is in the written text or where each fills the other's gaps. This is much harder to do than it looks, with the best leaving room for readers to make their own interpretations. Many popular and highly regarded series are complementary picturebooks: Beatrix Potter's *The Tale of Peter Rabbit* (Warne, 1902) and the many wonderful books that followed; the enchanting *Frog and Toad* stories by Arnold Lobel (HarperCollins, 1970); the gentle honesty of the *Frances* books by Russell and Lillian Hoban; and the tender *Little Bear* books by Else Holmelund Minarik and Maurice Sendak (HarperCollins, 1957–68). Old and young readers alike have been dazzled with the sheer inventiveness of the *Jolly Postman* series by Janet and Allan Ahlberg (Puffin, 1986–95) which, as well as being extremely funny and wonderfully creative in paper-engineering terms, plays with a wide variety of literacy artefacts (from advertisements to circulars and birthday cards), thereby familiarizing children with the way our culture works.

Below and right: Martin Waddell originally wrote a much longer text for this key spread in *Owl Babies*, where the tension is released as the mother returns to her chicks. In conversation with the authors of this book he revealed that, 'They were the best lines I ever wrote, but when I saw the image, I knew they were redundant.'

Much-loved, and often award-winning, individual picturebooks by the Ahlbergs and hugely talented illustrators are not always easy to categorize but they certainly involve words and pictures enhancing each other. In Eric Carle's *The Very Hungry Caterpillar* (World Publishing Company, 1969), for example, we can admire the colourful artwork that works so well with the delightful story, so beautifully crafted to engage young children. It was also one of the earliest examples of the inventive use of design and layout. *The Very Hungry Caterpillar* is now almost an industry in its own right; its huge sales over 40 years no doubt helped to enable the illustrator to set up the Eric Carle Museum of Picture Book Art in Amherst.

Writer Martin Waddell has collaborated successfully with a number of illustrators because of his particular sensitivity to the nature of pictorial text: for example, *Owl Babies* (Walker Books, 1992) with Patrick Benson, and the *Can't You Sleep, Little Bear?* series (Walker Books from 1994) with Barbara Firth. Waddell has talked about having to cut and change his original text in response to Benson's exceptional artwork and inspired vision in *Owl Babies.* The choices must have been the right ones as this picturebook quickly took on classic status with critics and children alike. The words tackle the timeless theme of separation anxiety in children with great warmth and simplicity while Benson's wonderfully textured, haunting nightscapes and appealing depiction of baby owls perfectly mirror, and add depth to, the narrative. Similarly, in the *Little Bear* series, words and pictures enhance each other beautifully

and it's the little details – Big Bear's sporting trophies on the mantelpiece, the photograph of his younger self hanging on the wall – that make the books so enjoyable for old and young readers alike. The language is repetitive and easy for children to anticipate, which is important in the early stages of reading, the artwork is gently traditional and the overall effect leaves a warm, reassuring glow.

Unfortunately, there is not space here to discuss the work of many other outstanding illustrators who deserve mention in this context – Michael Foreman, Mick Inkpen, Colin McNaughton, Jan Pienkowski and Nick Sharratt all fall into this category. In their picturebooks, word and image work together creatively to form a composite text, each enriching, expanding and enhancing the other. There are also edgier picturebooks that demand more of the reader and sometimes present the world in an uncomfortable or confusing way.

Some apparently simple picturebooks offer multiple interpretations. For example, less experienced readers can enjoy Ruth Brown's *Our Cat Flossie* (Dutton, 1986) as a funny story about a cat getting in the way of adults, while a more mature audience might notice the delicious exercise in irony. Helen Cooper's Kate Greenaway Medal-winning *The Baby Who Wouldn't Go to Bed* (Doubleday, 1996) explores with honesty, tenderness and psychological realism a wilful omnipotent infant in conflict with its mother. Here a straightforward text is accompanied by rich, strange, almost surreal imagery. Interestingly, this very picturebook is a favourite with many

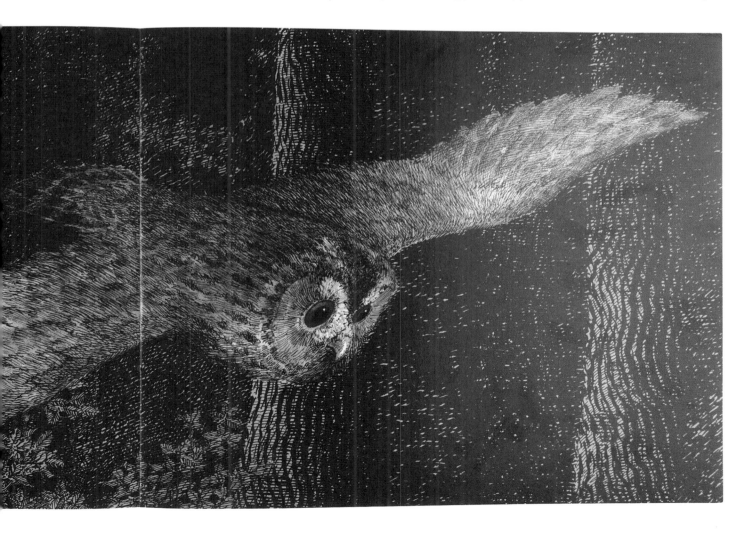

young children, which is perhaps not so surprising as reliable mother love is at the heart of the book.

Mother–child conflict is also the starting point for Maurice Sendak's *Where the Wild Things Are* (see p. 38), a picturebook that is the very model of excellence in word–picture interaction. The text is spare, concise, poetic. At the most powerful moment of action in the book, when fury and imagination merge, the words retreat so that three dynamic spreads are nothing but pictures. However, when our hero, Max, returns home, anger spent, to 'where someone loved him best of all', and his forbidden supper still awaits him, the closing words that signal that love transcends disagreements – 'and it was still hot' – make their impact against a white page. One of the reasons this book is a work of genius is because of the subtlety and vigour between word and image throughout.

Counterpoint and duet

Maria Nikolajeva and Carole Scott use the term 'counterpoint' when words and pictures tell different stories and provide 'alternative information or contradict each other in some way', resulting in several possible readings.[3] Philip Pullman, who is an expert on comics and graphic novels, as well as a well-

respected fantasy author, talks about counterpoint as 'the potential possessed by words and pictures in combination to "show different things happening at the same time"'.[4]

A picturebook that demonstrates counterpoint in action is Pat Hutchins' *Rosie's Walk* (HarperCollins, 1968), one of the first picturebooks to fully subvert the relationship between the 'seen' and the heard. The secret lies in what the words *don't* say as the fox is never mentioned in the written text which comprises a single sentence about Rosie, a confident little hen, taking a walk 'across the yard', 'around the pond', etc., then coming safely home. The fun comes from the fact that the fox, of whom Rosie appears to be unaware, has one misadventure after another as he chases after her. The book never fails to elicit pantomime squeals of 'Behind you!' in young children as they try to alert the hen to the danger. The reader never knows whether Rosie is very cool, very stupid or just plain lucky, but picturebooks like these provoke young readers to be actively involved in making meaning as they fill the gaps in for themselves. They may also provide children's first taste of irony in literature.

Satoshi Kitamura's *Lily Takes a Walk* (Corgi, 1987) is another good example of this 'duet'. Lily takes a happy stroll through city streets, blithely unaware of all the menacing terrors witnessed by her dog. Whenever he spies something

across the yard

dangerous, Lily is always looking the other way. The written text is entirely from Lily's point of view but the reader sees what the dog is seeing in the pictures (see pp. 78–79). A much more extreme case in point is David McKee's *I Hate My Teddy Bear*, which perplexes many adults as well as children with its surreal and strange pictures that have little apparent relationship to the written text.

John Burningham's *Shirley* books are also typical of counterpoint; the faint bleached verso pictures feature conventional parental concerns – 'be careful', 'don't do…' while the much more colourful recto reveals glorious adventures in the child's imagination. Burningham's classic, *Granpa* (Jonathan Cape, 1984), is also outstanding in the way he juxtaposes words and pictures. In this case, as in many of his picturebooks, the written text is based on 'conversation' between the protagonists, the words of each character being represented in different typefaces. But it's not quite that simple. Long before postmodernism was discussed in terms of picturebooks, Burningham was turning conventions upside down and leaving tantalizing gaps for the reader to fill. In *Granpa*, and in many of his other picturebooks, the grandfather and granddaughter don't have an actual dialogue; instead, the words are made up of those scraps of conversation that

sometimes go nowhere – such as questions that have no answers. For example, the pink embarrassed face of the little girl who has clearly made some sexual remark or sign accompanies the comment 'I didn't know teddy was another little girl'. Even more shocking is the yawning gap between the two characters, who turn their backs painfully on one another with the words 'That was not a nice thing to say to Granpa.' Every reader, and that includes every child reader, has been verbally unkind and most know how horrible it feels to have hurt someone. Burningham is the master of 'less is more'.

Burningham uses devices like sepia drawings and muted colours to suggest that granpa is becoming a bit fragile and is thinking about the past, even when his granddaughter is demanding his attention in the present – and, indeed, looking to the future. Occasionally, at most, the words hint at a change of status between the two, as when the little girl says 'You nearly slipped then, Granpa', and gives him a supporting hand. Most powerful of all is the final spread where the little girl, whose body posture is one of dejection, looks across at granpa's empty chair. Burningham leaves the reader to respond to the

---

3 Maria Nikolajeva and Carole Scott, *How Picturebooks Work*. Routledge, 2000.
4 David Lewis, *Reading Contemporary Picturebooks*. Routledge, 2001.

Opposite: Pat Hutchins' *Rosie's Walk* delights children with its use of the pantomime tradition. The central character is oblivious to the unseen fox's thwarted pursuit.

Below: David McKee's *I Hate My Teddy Bear* creates surreal visual landscapes with disparities of scale to disturb the readers' expectations of word–image relationships.

"I hate my teddy bear," said John.

"I hate my teddy bear," said Brenda.

image and interpret whether granpa has died or not. Children often come up with alternative explanations for his disappearance as they don't want to face the inevitability of death. Such picturebooks allow young readers that licence.

Most of these picturebooks offer young readers a chance to feel a bit bigger, older and wiser than the protagonists. Books such as these paved the way for the kind of postmodern picturebooks that are becoming familiar today, and which are rapidly defining themselves as an important new area of the visual arts. Chris Van Allsburg, Raymond Briggs, Emily Gravett, Peter Sis, Colin Thompson and David Wiesner are excellent exponents of postmodern picturebooks.[5]

---

[5] We have refrained from mentioning those whose individual books are considered elsewhere in this volume.

Below: John Burningham's *Granpa* is visual literature at its best. Never afraid of ambiguity, the author leaves room for the reader to fill in large gaps between word and image.

This is a lovely chocolate ice-cream.

It's not chocolate, it's strawberry.

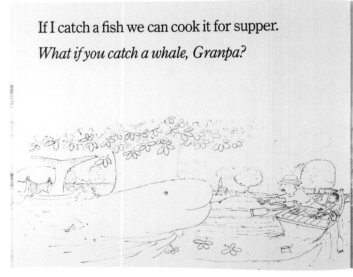

If I catch a fish we can cook it for supper.

What if you catch a whale, Granpa?

Wordless books and graphic novels

As we have shown, all challenging picturebooks make readers work hard (though it's enjoyable toil) at filling in the gaps between the words and pictures to construct meaning. The wordless variety require young readers to create the text for themselves, providing what Anne Rowe calls 'voices off': 'The events may seem to tell themselves but they are given voice by a reader/narrator.' She goes on to point out that the narrator (illustrator) who directs the telling appears invisible and is supplemented by the reader's 're-creation of the implied text'.[6] We begin, therefore, by disabusing readers of any preconceived ideas about these books being simple – or even completely wordless as they all have titles. Many of the best of this genre are extremely complex and sophisticated. Quentin Blake's *Clown* (Jonathan Cape, 1995) is a good example, as many careful 'readings' are required to make sense of this painful and tender story. Even wordless picturebooks for a young age, such as Jan Ormerod's *Sunshine* (Kestrel, 1981) and *Moonlight* (Harmondsworth, 1982), and Monique Félix's *Little Mouse* books (Moonlight Publishing, various dates), require assiduous

[6] From Styles, Bearne & Watson, '*Voices Off*'. Cassell, 1996.

Right: Wordless picturebooks require detailed planning, as the author becomes director, stage manager and actor in a theatrical production. This sequence is from Quentin Blake's *Clown*.

observation to understand what is happening and to get all the jokes. Raymond Briggs' *The Snowman* (Hamish Hamilton, 1978) is now a classic animation but it started life as an exquisitely told visual story for six-year-olds and younger which, for all its tremendous vitality and fun, is about the inevitability of loss. Shirley Hughes' *Up and Up* (The Bodley Head, 1979) is a tour de force that requires painstaking attention on the part of the reader to pick up all the threads.

Serious issues as well as fun are frequently tackled in wordless books. Jeannie Baker's *Window* (Julia MacRae, 1991) was one of the first picturebooks to tackle the destruction of the environment head-on without using a single word. Istvan Banyai, Philippe Dupasquier, Peter Collington, David Wiesner and, of course, Mitsumasa Anno are other great exponents of this genre. Banyai in particular has taken the wordless book to new levels with his ability to subvert the very nature of the image as a two-dimensional representation of three-dimensional form. In *Zoom* (Viking, 1995), he plays with our inherent assumptions when reading visual text by cleverly setting up expectations before undermining and disturbing them.

In *Um Dia Na Praia* (*A Day at the Beach*, Planeta Tangerina, 2008) Bernardo Carvalho also plays wordless visual tricks by using simple, toneless flat colours and the sophisticated handling of space to give visual clues in almost pictogram form – taking the viewer's eyes and mind on a journey full of surprises and aesthetic harmony. Wordless picturebooks are emerging as an increasingly common form of visual literature and, of course, have the great benefit of being universally readable.

The growth in interest in graphic novels in recent years has had considerable impact on children's picturebooks. In some instances, the boundaries between these and sequential 'comic strip' art have become blurred: the use of multiple framed images and speech bubbles for four- to seven-year-olds is increasingly commonplace. Shaun Tan's *The Arrival* (Lothian, 2007) has been particularly influential as it is wordless, sequential and difficult to pin down in terms of target audience. Such crossover books can cause problems for booksellers, who are often confused about where to place them. Tan himself states that such considerations cannot be uppermost in the artist's mind when making a book:

Left and opposite: In *Um Dia Na Praia* flat colour without line is used with careful attention to the placement of every element in order to develop a wordless text. The very simple shapes need to carry the entire weight of a subtle pictorial narrative.

It often doesn't set out to appeal to a predefined audience but rather to build one for itself. The artist's responsibility lies first and foremost with the work itself, trusting that it will invite the attention of others by the force of its conviction.[7]

A more mainstream, but nonetheless original, example is Jason Chapman's *Stan and Mabel* (Templar, 2010). Chapman, who combines book-making with a role as artist in residence at the Battersea Dogs Home in London, uses a melange of sequential structures to create a hybrid of road movie and picturebook.

---

[7] http://www.shauntan.net/essay1.html

Pictorial text

We lived beneath the mat,
Warm and snug and fat.
But one woe, and that
Was the cat !
To our joys
a clog, In
our eyes a
fog, On our
hearts a log
Was the dog !
When the
cat's away
Then
the mice
will
play.
But, alas !
one day (so they say)
Came the dog and
cat. Hunting
for a
rat
Crushed
the mice
all flat,
Each
one
as
he
sat
Underneath the mat, Warm and snug
and fat.
Think of that.

Above: Lewis Carroll's *The Mouse's Tale* is an early example of text taking the visual form of that which it describes or alludes to.

The blurring of boundaries between text as the representation of something visual and text as a pictorial element in itself is not new. Lewis Carroll's *The Mouse's Tale* has been described as the first concrete poem; the text exists in the shape of a tail and plays on the tale/tail spelling. In other words, it is formatted to visually resemble its theme. El Lissitzky's use of letterforms as characters is another well-known example.

In *Art and Text* (Black Dog, 2009) Will Hill writes:

To give text a pictorial form reveals complex contradictions between visual representation and linguistic description, and reminds us that language is a fragile and illogical construct, bound to its subject by cultural compact alone. While we take for granted the equivalence between the word and its subject, they are not linked by any actual resemblance, but only by the shared perception of meaning inherent in language.

Hill also quotes Stefan Themerson who, in collaboration with his artist wife Franciszka, wrote and published a number of influential picturebooks from the 1940s:

Language is one species of the genus sign and pictorial representations are another species of the same genus. These two species can be wedded to one another. They can be wedded, either politely and comfortably (as when an illustration is wedded to a text or a caption to a drawing) or they can start an illicit liaison, so intimately integrated that one doesn't know anymore who is the bride and who is the bridegroom.

As the merging of pictorial and verbal text has become increasingly commonplace, more and more artists have taken control of the overall design of the page. Hand-lettering has become more common, even though this presents problems for publishers in terms of printing foreign language co-editions (traditionally, it has been a rule of thumb that picturebook text is black so that only this colour is reprinted in foreign language editions, thereby saving costs).

An example of the 'new wave' of picturebook makers is Oliver Jeffers. Originally from Northern Ireland, Jeffers is now based in Brooklyn, New York. His understanding of the creative potential of the picturebook is particularly acute. His books have become increasingly sophisticated yet are always entirely accessible. This is at least partly because of his particular sensitivity to word–image interplay. Speaking about his work,[8] he stressed the fact that the relationship between word and image is central to his work in its various contexts, including paintings for exhibition in art galleries.

I don't call myself a picturebook writer or illustrator. I use the term 'picturebook maker'. When writer and illustrator are different people, I suppose texts are given to the artist in a fully formed state. But I do both and the two will evolve together. Sometimes the pictures can inform the words rather than the other way around. Often it's easier for me to not say something in words. I show it rather than say it.

In recent books such as *The Great Paper Caper* and *The Heart and the Bottle* (HarperCollins, 2008 and 2010 respectively), Jeffers has increasingly experimented with structure. By his own admission, *The Great Paper Caper* owes something to the TV detective Columbo in that it turns the traditional whodunnit on its head by revealing the guilty party at the outset. Thereafter, we follow the various characters affected by the crime in their efforts to identify the perpetrator. Jeffers' masterly use of pictorial space is another key to the book's success. Superficially, his oeuvre as a gallery artist may seem to be very different from his book work. In fact, concerns with spatial relationships and the ways word and image interact are central to both strands of his work but are articulated differently.

The following case studies look at contemporary artists who are at the cutting edge of the art of picturebook-making. For all of them, the interplay between word and image is central to their creative practice.

---

[8] In conversation with Martin Salisbury, Association of Illustrators Forum, March 2010.

Below: Stefan and Franciszka Themerson were influential writers, thinkers, artists and film-makers who published books through their Gaberbocchus Press. Stefan's pertinent observations on the potential relationships between word and image were ahead of their time. *My First Nursery Book* has recently been reissued by Tate Publishing (London, 2008).

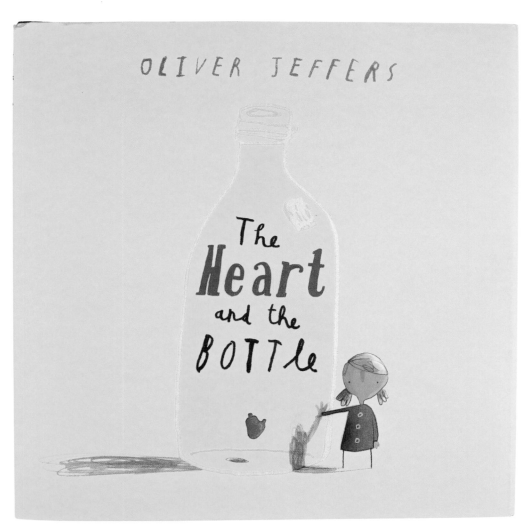

...until the day she found an empty chair.

Left and below: *The Heart and the Bottle* by Oliver Jeffers. The interplay between word and image plays a key role in Jeffers' output as both picturebook maker and gallery artist.

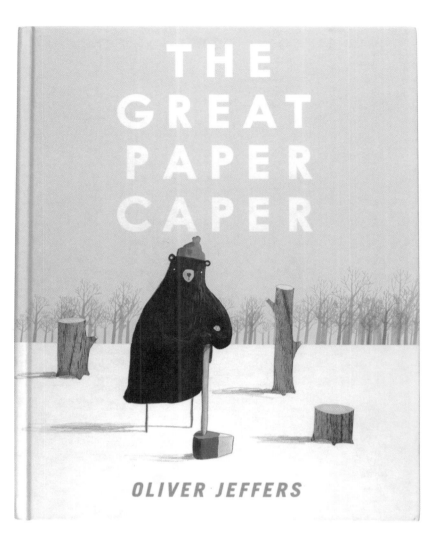

Left and below: Oliver Jeffers takes the extensive textual information on the copyright page of *The Great Paper Caper* and forms it into a tree motif in keeping with the theme of the book, blurring the boundaries between text and image.

Professional case study: Author and illustrator collaboration

Vladimir Radunsky and Chris Raschka
Hip Hop Dog

An interesting aspect of the ongoing collaborations between Vladimir Radunsky and Chris Raschka is that they are both artists and they are both writers. The traditional concept of writers coming up with ideas and illustrators visualizing them does not apply here. This is a genuine meeting of minds where projects emerge and evolve with fluctuating creative dynamics.

In the 1970s, Radunsky studied at the Moscow Architectural Institute, one of the descendants of the legendary Vkhutemas studios set up by Lenin in the 1920s 'to prepare master artists of the highest qualifications for industry, and builders and managers for professional-technical education'. He says his education was of a very classical nature: six years of formal drawing, painting and architecture. This, he feels, was an important foundation for him creatively.

I have never felt restricted or 'locked in' by this rigorous training. I never felt 'This is what I'm going to do for the rest of my life'. I still think architecture is the best training in the creative arts. But at that time in Russia, I couldn't see any future for myself as an architect. It was the time of the 'paper architects', such as Alexander Brodsky, when the best architectural work existed only on paper. All of the graduates pursued anything but architecture – music, design, etc.

Radunsky left Russia in 1982 and worked in New York where he designed art books, working for clients such as the Metropolitan Museum of Art, Abbeville and Marlborough Gallery.

Below and opposite: Vladimir Radunsky's swirling vortex of type and image perfectly complements Chris Raschka's rap text in *Hip Hop Dog*.

I always liked children's books. In Russia it was an area of escape and relative creative freedom, free from oppression. There is a wonderful tradition of Russian illustrated books. The collaborations of writers and artists such as Samuil Marshak and Vladimir Lebedev, for instance. Even in Stalin's time there were avant-garde poets and artists working in children's books. I always respected this tradition but didn't get involved in making books until I arrived in the US. It happened by accident really. An illustrator (Robert Rayevsky) invited me to design one of his picturebooks. I became so involved in the design that I think I started taking over his book without realizing it. So then I started making my own books. I suppose my particular way into picturebooks was one of not understanding any separation between word and image or between design and illustration. When I am the author, I do everything – except my wife translates my English into English.

The initial idea for *Hip Hop Dog* (HarperCollins NY, 2010) was Radunsky's. Chris Raschka is a highly successful writer, artist and musician. The two had collaborated on a number of books with great success but, rather than signing a binding deal with the publishers, they chose to make theirs an informal arrangement, and agreed to come together when an idea inspired them. Radunsky says:

We didn't want to be tied down. In a way, we work like partisans. We do jam sessions together and the outcome is a book. I had the idea to do a hip hop book for children. But I couldn't do it. I don't have the language! It needed some space between real hip hop and this hip hop – a different vocabulary. So I asked Chris if he would write it. I just gave him the character of the dog really. I didn't want to restrict him.

In *Hip Hop Dog* Radunsky takes Raschka's words and creates integrated page designs where the visual shape, weight and direction of the words is as important to the page as the characters that share the space. The text sits on roughly cut panels, with extra weight given to the words that need to be emphasized to express the rhythms of the rap. Sometimes the panels fall away gradually; sometimes they spiral into the centre of the page, requiring the reader to spin the book rapidly in order to maintain the meter of the poetry.

Radunsky's love of words is clear. He has also worked with the late American Poet Laureate, Joseph Brodsky: 'He came to my studio and told me he was going to write a book for me'; and has illustrated work by another of his favourite writers, Edward Lear, whose writing, he says 'makes me feel like I wrote it'.

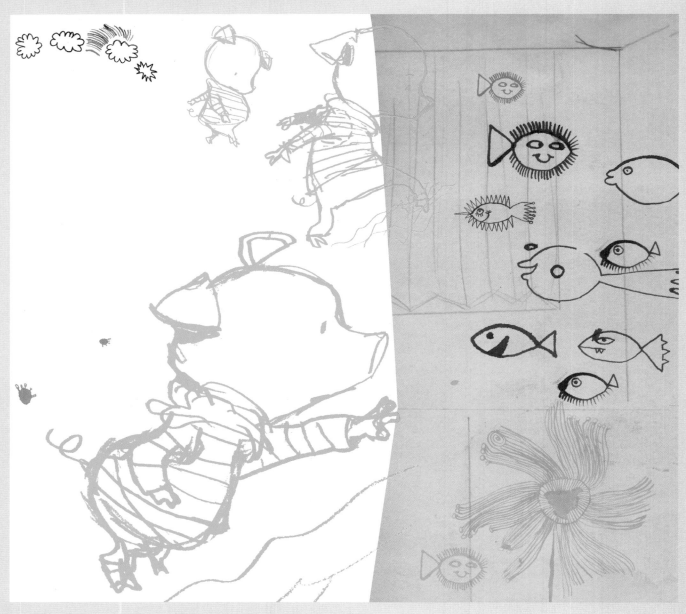

—Hello, I'm Pink Piglet.—
—So I see.—
—I'd like to be green. Do you think I could be as green as you?—
asked Pig Piglet nervously.
—Definitely not! I'm an exceptional shade of green and either
you have it or you don't. There's nothing you can do about it.—

With that the frog blew up like a balloon. Then she
turned round so that Pink Piglet could get the full view.
The next thing Pink Piglet knew there was a splash and
suddenly two thin red legs appeared out of nowhere.

Professional case study: Designer and illustrator collaboration

Marcin Brykcynski (text), Joanna Olech and Marta Ignerska (illustration), Marta Ignerska (design)
Pink Piglet

Pink Piglet was originally published in Polish by Wydawnictwo Znac in 2006; the publisher of the English-language edition was WingedChariot Press, which has attempted to introduce a number of European picturebooks to the English-speaking market. The book describes Pink Piglet's moment of dissatisfaction about being Pink Piglet, and his subsequent journey across the fields to encounter all the other animals whose identities seem infinitely preferable to his own. A final encounter with a chameleon reassures Piglet that being pink may not be so bad after all. It's a common theme but one that is addressed with a particularly adventurous use of the page. Once again, we see design and illustration merging to make visual text. In this instance the designer and illustrator are not the same person, but the designer's work adds meaning to the page and plays a crucial part in the creation of the page. So much so that Marta Ignerska is credited as both designer and co-illustrator.

Ignerska reassembled Joanna Olech's drawings digitally along with the text to create pages that are teeming with movement, life and narrative meaning. The original Polish version is a large-scale hardback edition which projects the full impact of the sprawling sketchbook effect of the pages. WingedChariot's Neal Hoskins explains that some compromises were necessary for the English-language market:

We had to change the font from the one used in the Polish edition but we tried to stay true to the feel of it. And where the text appears in pink we made the colour a little more intense. It was felt that there might be a legibility problem. The English-language market is more used to a standard black font and this might be too difficult to follow. Having said that, since the book was published there has been more experimentation with the visual side of text through people like Oliver Jeffers. We were drawn to this book for a number of reasons, the unique colour palette, for instance, and the 'unfinished' look.

Ignerska also took control of the scale of the drawings: Olech provided the raw ingredients which were then composed and arranged at differing levels of reduction and enlargement. It is interesting to speculate about what the results would have been had designer–artists of the 1950s and 1960s, such as Paul Rand, had access to similar digital collage methods.

Opposite: *Pink Piglet* is the result of collaboration between a number of artists and designers, which results in a complex fusion of word and image that breaks free from normal conventions about the relationship between the two. Sketchbook character studies are resized and reorganized to give texture to the page.

Student case study: Exploiting word–image disparity

Marta Altés
No!

No! was developed by Marta Altés about halfway through her studies for her masters in children's book illustration at Cambridge School of Art. Having studied visual sequence in the previous module, she was eager to experiment with the picturebook format and, in particular, to explore the potential for word–image disparity and playful counterpoint. After toying with a number of ideas, she settled on one that exploits the gap in understanding between a dog and his owner. Based on the artist's own dog, the character narrates his story, and explains to the reader his perception of the world and his place within it. At the beginning of the sequence, he introduces himself, 'Hi, I'm "No"'. Altés explains:

When I started thinking about this story, I wanted to explain how my dog was growing up, and how he was not doing naughty things any more. And trying to resolve the ending of this story, I started wondering what he could be thinking about when he was being so naughty… Sometimes dogs do bad things because they are playing, because they are angry with us or simply because they are dogs. Then I thought it could be funny to imagine the story from the dog's point of view, and imagine that dogs do these things because what they really want is to help us. While they are 'helping' us they can hear us

Below and opposite: Images and storyboards from Marta Altés' *No!*

shouting to them 'Don't!', 'No!', 'Get out!' and so on. So I imagined that maybe they think that this is their name. And they feel very proud helping us.

In the book we know what the dog thinks from the text, while what we are seeing is an image of him being naughty. This combination, the text and the image telling us different things, makes it possible to have two different points of view, two realities – the dog's and the reader's – at the same time. This makes the book funnier because you can see this contradiction between them. The images give more story, one that is not explained by words.

Throughout the 32 pages, the dog describes to the reader the various helpful services he performs for his owners. These include tasting their food to check it is OK, digging for treasure in the garden, and taking the washing off the line. Accompanying the image of each of these activities is a speech bubble from out of frame containing the increasingly desperate exclamation 'Nooo!'.

Of course, the previous paragraph perfectly illustrates the clunky limitations of words alone as a means of expressing the humour of this idea. But the elegance of the outcome of the project is achieved through carefully considered editing of

pictures and words. We are able to experience the world from the dog's misguided viewpoint; we hear his version of events while we see what the despairing owner sees. There is no need for us to see a pictorial representation of the owner. All we need is to hear the voice from 'offstage'.

For the picturebook maker, having a clever idea is one thing, but planning it out carefully and structuring it to fit neatly within a given number of pages (usually 32) is not easy. The storyboarding process is essential in order to allow the artist to see how well the word–image balance is working. The drawings are often kept very basic, so that the charm and vitality of the work is not left behind at this stage and also to ensure that the creation of final artwork does not become simply a deadening copying process. Altés tries to draw as directly as possible on to the finished artwork, but in doing this she has to be sure that the positioning of the text has been carefully considered before the drawings are made. All this is done at the storyboarding stage.

Below: Image from Marta Altés' *No!*

Chapter 5

SUITABLE FOR CHILDREN?

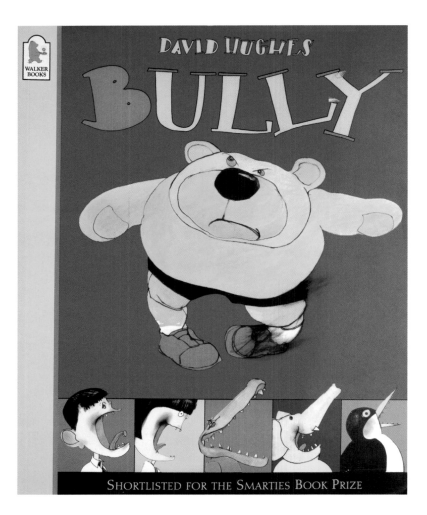

Perceptions of suitable or appropriate content[1] for children's picturebooks have changed greatly over the years. They also vary considerably across cultures today. It is something of a paradox that, while the marketing departments of many publishing houses in the West insist that picturebooks come with clearly labelled, target audience ages, many artists and authors are creating crossover books (even these need to be named and labelled) that can appeal to different age groups on different levels. The picturebook as a medium of communication for all ages is an increasingly evident and welcome phenomenon, albeit one that can cause problems for booksellers in terms of where to place the books on their shelves. The CJ Picture Book Festival in South Korea celebrates this emerging trend and states in its publicity material:

Picture books, in the present era, enjoy a status as a culture form to be enjoyed by people of all ages. It is a precious and versatile art that has already left the confines of paper behind, shattering the boundaries of its own genre and fusing with various other forms of art and imagery.[2]

How do we as adults decide what is 'suitable' for children? Early children's stories, including many fairy tales, were often extremely savage and dark in their cautionary nature. While difficult subjects, such as death, illness, abuse and racism have been tackled in children's literature over the last 50 years, many commentators – particularly in the West – have increasingly come to believe that young children must be protected from all things unpleasant and dangerous, in both life and literature. It could be argued that this perception extends to all walks of life in our contemporary risk-averse culture. And although domestic violence, dying, sex and relationships, sadness and war have all been explored in the pages of the picturebook, some feel that childhood has become more and more sentimentalized in certain areas of visual and verbal literature. Nevertheless, there are many cultures where discussing the less cosy aspects of life (and death) in picturebooks is more commonplace than it is elsewhere, along with a reluctance to specify a target audience age – notably in Scandinavia, other parts of mainland Europe such as France, Belgium and Germany, and in the Far East, especially South Korea. In the United Kingdom, however, publishers have tended to allow difficult subjects only in works by more well-known authors such as John Burningham, David McKee and Quentin Blake – those with a long track record of sales who are seen as having earned the right to make what are regarded as more risky books. It is less easy to generalize about the United States, Canada and Australia, where there are many forces at play across a wide range of publishing houses. On the one hand, edgy, highly experimental books are being published in all these countries, but on the other – particularly in the United States – the conservative force of the Christian right is a countervailing influence.

The reasons for these differences are too numerous to consider here, but attitudes to, and perceptions of, childhood are highly significant. We know that the notion of childhood is socially constructed and varies over time and across cultures. No book is ever socially or politically neutral, and books for the young are especially sensitive to the way a particular culture, at a specific time, views childhood. The United States is an interesting case in point, as the ideologies of, for example, downtown New York and rural West Virginia, are poles apart – but the former has more influential publishing houses. And, of course, social mores vary greatly between societies. In the context of picturebooks, this affects the extent to which it is acceptable to discuss uncomfortable subjects openly. Aesthetic sensibilities also come into play, and are influenced by each country's unique historical traditions in the graphic, decorative and fine arts.

The stylistic suitability of visual texts for children is an equally subjective and contentious matter. Many publishers and commentators express views about the suitability or otherwise of artworks for children, yet there is no definitive research that can tell us what kind of imagery is most appealing or communicative to the young eye.[3] The perceived wisdom is that bright, primary colours are most effective for the very young. The difficulty is that children of traditional picturebook age tend not to have the language skills to express in words what they are receiving from an image. They can also be suggestible and prone to saying what they imagine adults want to hear. So, even with the best designed research projects, the world that children are experiencing will inevitably remain something of a mystery to us. As adults we make decisions on their behalf, even though we may struggle to retain the magical ability to read pictures that appears to come so naturally to the young.

This chapter looks at the varying ways some taboo subjects have been approached in children's picturebooks, with examples from a number of different countries.

---

[1] 'Content' refers here to both subject matter and the stylistic nature of the pictorial texts that convey it.

[2] www.cjbook.org/english/about/introduce.php

[3] There has been some research into children's preferred art styles, such as *Children's Preferences in Picture Story Book Variables* (Ruth Helen Amsden, 1960) and *Effect of Art Style on Children's Picture Preferences* (Inez L. Ramsey, 1982).

Left: Katje Vermeire's artwork for *Mare en de Dingen* (text Tine Mortier; De Eenhoorn, 2009) sensitively explores the subject of ageing and death.

Er moest van alles geregeld worden. Moeder belde, schreef,
rende en snoot haar neus in duizend zakdoekjes.
Mare ging naar grootmoe. Grootmoes ogen werden nat, en
daarna ook haar wangen en haar jurk. Mare had geen handen
genoeg om al dat water tegen te houden.
Straks staat de hele kamer onder water!
De vloer werd nat. Zo meteen zou het bed naar buiten drijven.
Dan varen we naar Engeland.

Violence

The Norwegian husband and wife team, artist Svein Nyhus and writer Gro Dahle, are well known for creating picturebooks that deal with uncomfortable themes. *Sinna Mann* (Angry Man, Cappelen, 2003) deals with domestic violence. A close working relationship between author and artist allows words and pictures to synthesize in a harrowing portrayal of the build-up of tension in the domestic environment. The growing anger of the father is described visually by the use of scale. Through the pages, the father gets bigger and bigger in relation to the mother and child. His explosive anger is reflected in burning colours. Nyhus uses visual devices such as sharp objects perched precariously on the edge of surfaces to give a heightened sense of impending violence. He says of the audience for this book:

The audience is mainly children, especially those who have experienced domestic violence and parents with mental illness. These children's books may be classified as allalderlitteratur in Norwegian, i.e. 'literature for all ages', a crossover genre, as it also has a psychological and symbolic side, which is best understood by adults. So the books have at least two levels; the concrete what-you-see aimed at children, and a deeper or higher meaning aimed at adults. The text is poetic and symbolic with a lot of verbal metaphors but also contains quotations from people with similar problems.

Right and opposite: Svein Nyhus and Gro Dahle's *Sinna Mann* uses exaggerated extremes of scale and colour to emphasize the simmering anger of the father and the vulnerability of the wife and child in this exploration of domestic violence.

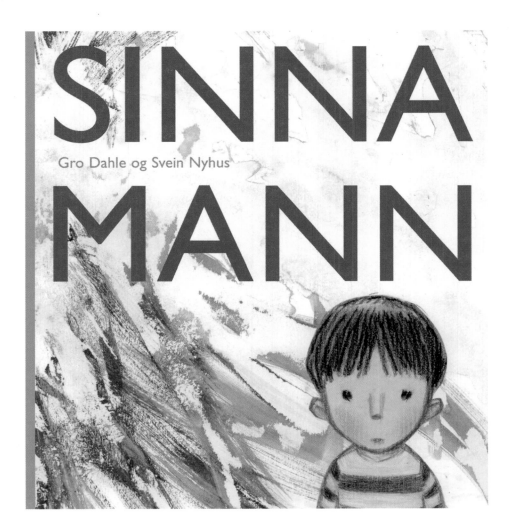

Asked why he feels a picturebook was the appropriate medium for addressing such a topic, Nyhus says:

Sinna Mann *was made in response to a request from a family therapist needing a simple book about children witnessing domestic violence to use as a 'conversation piece' in his talks with his clients, both children, women and men. I think he initially wanted an information book that ideally should have the potential of 'saving the world from all evil'. We could only 'offer' an artistically free fiction book as we thought the educational twist may subdue or weaken the content and impact. So this is our (i.e. my wife Gro Dahle's and my) way of trying to solve his challenge. The book has by no means become a sales hit, of course, but it has generated a lot of reaction and even been adapted into some theatrical plays and an animated film. I also think there is a slightly provocative or sensational effect when combining disturbing subjects with traditionally nice and cute children's literature. This may have helped making such serious matters more visible in the media and the public debate.*

In *Håret til Mamma* (Mum's Hair, Cappelen, 2007) they explore the issue of a parent's depression from the perspective of the child. The mother's hair is used as a visual metaphor; it becomes increasingly entangled as the situation deteriorates, and the child movingly tries to 'comb out' the depression.

Håret til Mamma was also a job initiated by a therapist. As with Sinna Mann *we had free hands to write and illustrate it like an ordinary and 'normal' children's book. The Norwegian government's generous financial support for new quality literature in Norwegian makes it possible to publish narrow titles without taking commercial success etc. into consideration. This way Norwegian illustrators, writers and publishers can experiment a little bit more than foreign colleagues may do.*

Nyhus tends to work mainly in children's books nowadays, but previously worked for newspapers as a caricaturist and cartoonist. Clearly, he has found a natural canvas in the picturebook:

A picturebook is in many ways like a gallery wall to me, with lots of space and room to fill with my illustrations. It also has the qualities of a stage with scenography making it a small universe of its own, so to speak. I have a lot of ideas and great optimism and energy when beginning a book project, but always end up totally exhausted and frustrated with my own insufficient talent and ineffective ways of doing things.

As for the difficult issue of whether the picturebook can reach a broader audience than the traditional three- to seven-year-old readership, Nyhus is optimistic:

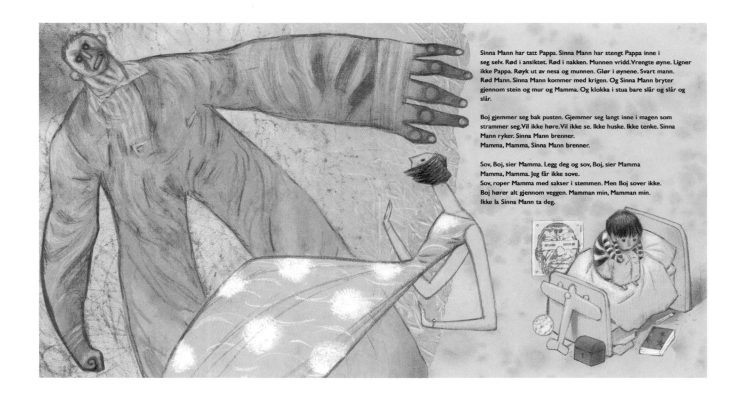

It is, of course, a matter of definitions. If you mean 'books with pictures' there already are a lot of them. I think the new generations mix visual culture, both popular and more serious, for children and adults alike, much more freely than before. Then there also becomes a commercial potential for books aimed at 'all ages'. Picturebooks for children are usually read aloud by adults for small children, and it is a good trick to make something for the adults as well – and not bore them with exclusively children's material. Both target groups need something to make them interested, I think. But this broad appeal and richness is, of course, a quality found in all great literature.

We have been a couple for almost 30 years, making books together since 1993. Gro's intuitive and poetic creativity has stimulated my more analytic approach and traditional style and helped me develop it in a more experimental direction. A good combination of different natures, I think.

Reactions in English-speaking countries to books such as those of Dahle and Nyhus can be extreme. Some people are outraged at the idea of exposing children to their subject matter; other people (often artists and educators) despair that such books are not more widely available.

Below and opposite: In *Håret til Mamma* Nyhus and Dahle approach another sensitive issue – depression – through the visual metaphor of tangled hair.

Men Emma er modig.
Hun finner børsten i skuffen
og begynner å børste håret til Mamma.

Emma børster og børster
til krøllene brøler,
til tustene freser,
til flokene bruser.

HÅRET TIL MAMMA

GRO DAHLE &
SVEIN NYHUS

CAPPELEN

Below and opposite: *Welhavens Vase* could be considered a picturebook for adults; there are no children in its cast and the storyline deals with the triumph of love over material possession. But the intricate visual detail appeals on many levels.

Love
and sex

Bjorn Rune Lie's *Welhavens Vase* (Magicon, Norway, 2010) is a touching tale of a love that blossoms in unlikely circumstances. Welhaven, a wealthy, haughty man finds himself forced to travel in the company of a lowly truck driver when he moves his valuable possessions from one mansion to an even larger one he has acquired. He clings to his priceless Ming dynasty vase as the kindly driver chats to him. Along the way, they encounter a circus troupe, stuck at the side of the road because their truck has terminally broken down. To Welhaven's horror, the driver offers to take the troupe to its destination so that the show can go on. Welhaven falls for the contortionist and, to cut a long story short, eventually has to free her from the interior of the priceless vase by smashing it – the perfect metaphor for Welhaven's release from his own entrapment by material possessions.

As a picturebook, *Welhavens Vase* could be said to break many of the suitability rules that tend to apply to the more commercial end of the market. There are no children in evidence, and the visual and verbal texts do not make any overt concessions to an audience in the usual three- to seven-year-old age bracket. Many of the feelings and emotions expressed could be said to be primarily adult – yet the underlying message that it is important to put people ahead of possessions is a universal one. Some publishers may argue that the busy, painterly visual text is too complex for the young reader. The artist's keen interest in letterforms and graphic motifs certainly makes each page a complex fusion of word and image that is challenging for the younger child. But this is a picturebook that can be enjoyed by all ages, one that succeeds on many different levels. The story can be read out loud to the youngest children but is also filled with subtle visual references that will only register with the adult reader. Asked whether he considered the book suitable for children, Bjorn Rune Lie says:

An illustrated book tends to become a 'children's book' by default, but I normally refer to my books as 'picturebooks', because I want adults to appreciate them too. Children and 'childish adults' was the age range!

I guess the book does deal with adult concepts to an extent; love, loneliness, consumerism, class, etc. All the characters are adults. I wanted to do a book about a trucker, and when I started working on ideas, it just became set in an adult world. I got cold feet about the story at one point and did a whole new version with a boy as the protagonist, but my publishers ditched it. In the end I just tried to remember what fascinated me when I was young. My favourite books when I was little were the Serafin books by Philippe Fix. They had a lot of adult references in them which went over my head, but I absolutely loved them. The drawings are amazing!

'Style' wise I just did my own thing with this book, just trying to experiment and have fun. I was more interested in doing something I liked than trying to appeal to the sensibilities of a specific target audience. A bit self-indulgent perhaps, but it was for a small independent publisher who wanted to push things a bit.

Death and sadness

Over the years many artists and authors have attempted to tackle the subject of mortality in picturebooks. Of course, death in its generalized sense often crops up in books for the young, but using the subject as the central theme of a picturebook is a very different matter. The natural, insatiable curiosity of the young mind will always want to know more, especially about subjects parents may be inclined to avoid. In the developed world, for better or worse, many people are choosing to have children later in life. This means that instances of children of picturebook age experiencing the loss of a grandparent are becoming increasingly common.

Approaches to the subject of death have been many and varied. Most commonly perhaps, it is dealt with through a much-loved pet dying and a reassuring representation of heaven, where everyone is having a lovely time and looking down benignly and comfortably on our worldly travails. A rather different approach can be found in Wolf Erlbruch's *Duck, Death and the Tulip*, which was first published in Germany in 2007 as *Ente, Tod und Tulpe*. The book follows Duck as he nears the end of his life and becomes aware of Death – depicted in uncompromising form as a clothed skeleton – following him. 'Who are you? What are you up to, creeping along behind me?' asks Duck at the beginning of the book. 'Good,' comes

Below and opposite: The bleak, uncompromising visual and verbal text of Wolf Erlbruch's *Duck, Death and the Tulip*.

They could see the pond far below.
There it lay, so still – and so lonely.
That's what it will be like when I'm dead, Duck thought.
The pond alone, without me.

the reply, 'You finally noticed me. I am Death.' The pages of the book are sparsely populated, on a white background, and consists largely of the ensuing philosophical dialogue between Duck and her follower. When Duck eventually feels cold and lies lifeless, Death carries her to the water, gently places a tulip (which has hitherto provided a rare splash of warm colour on the pages) on Duck and nudges her on her way.

Many people, particularly in the English-language publishing world, may see books such as *Duck, Death and Tulip* as a form of vanity publishing, indicative of the different, northern European attitude to death, and published to win awards for artistic brilliance and sensitivity. It certainly provides an extreme contrast to some of the over-sentimental picturebooks published in the English-speaking world. Opinions differ over whether such a book has a place in a children's bookshop. Erlbruch himself has strong views. He bemoans what he describes as 'the pinky aesthetics in English picturebooks', and speculates that this may be both a cultural and a marketing phenomenon. 'Where have all the Tenniels and Shepards gone?' he asks in despair. Asked whether he thinks English-speaking children are being deprived of quality visual literature by marketing perceptions, he says: 'Absolutely so. Their childhood is being stolen by the rubbish given to them by their marketing-and-telly-conditioned parents!' Erlbruch never consciously considers his audience when he creates books, though he hopes to initiate a dialogue between parents and children: '… a thing which has become rare nowadays in a more or less speechless society.'

Sunkyung Cho's *Blue Bird* (Yellow Stone, 2009) deals with the complex emotional issues of parent–child relationships, growing up and independence. Word and image come together to create a somewhat harrowing exploration of the ultimate love of a parent: 'letting go' and releasing her offspring only through her own death. Printed in two colours – black plus the blue of the bird – the book speaks in a poetic tone with no trace of sentimentality. Although it was inspired by a deep personal experience, the artist explains that he hopes it has wide appeal:

Individuality exists based on age, gender, and background but as human beings like any other, there also exists some form of emotional homogeneity. In addition, despite this work taking on a personal theme, it has universal appeal because it includes all the basic emotional elements that all humans share. I don't believe that explaining emotionally complex issues to children is easy, but children are well capable of experiencing an array

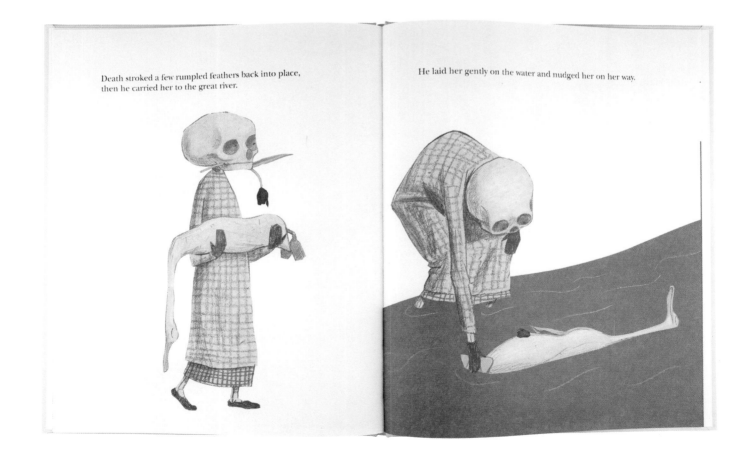

Death stroked a few rumpled feathers back into place, then he carried her to the great river.

He laid her gently on the water and nudged her on her way.

of universal human emotions. They may lack in life experiences, but they too can take part in sharing these complexities of emotions if we respect them as fellow beings that can think and reason.

Sunkyung Cho hopes picturebooks will increasingly appeal to adults: 'If picturebooks exist with contents and level that are appropriate for adults, I believe them to be another important means of communication.'

The Sad Book (Walker Books, 2004), written by the popular poet Michael Rosen (Children's Laureate 2007–09), and illustrated by Quentin Blake, takes a painful and honest look at depression, death and grieving. The book is based on his son's sudden death as a late teenager, and Rosen writes in the first person about everything from feeling that people will avoid him if he shows his sadness to moments of utter despair, mixed with happy memories of his son, accounts of trying to cope, the kindness of friends and, at the end, a little bit of hope. The

low-key but devastating darkness of parts of the written text is brilliantly mirrored in Blake's illustrations; overwhelmingly grey with a few telling, scratchy pen-and-ink lines, they depict utter misery. Blake is also good at lifting the mood with a touch of yellow, an exuberant child character, a toy raising an eyebrow to the reader, a flickering candle flame. From its murky cover with bits of rubbish strewn around a city street, to its unrelentingly grey endpapers, the book's treatment of some of the toughest emotions human beings ever suffer is frank, straightforward and true to life. It was critically acclaimed in the West and may have gone some way to breaking down the barriers outlined above.

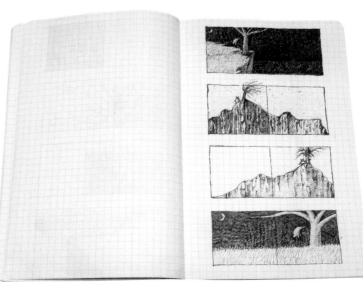

Opposite: Sunkyung Cho's *Blue Bird* was developed from a deeply personal perspective on relationships between parents and children. The first notebook compositions shown here already demonstrate the intensity of vision that is retained in the final version.

Below: Michael Rosen's and Quentin Blake's *The Sad Book* was one of the most high-profile books to deal with the subject of death.

Sometimes this makes me really angry.
I say to myself, "How dare he go and die like that?
How dare he make me sad."

He doesn't say anything,
because he's not there any more.

Man's inhumanity to man

Very different approaches to the broad subject of wars and racial tension can be seen in Armin Greder's award-winning *The Island* (first published in Germany by Saurlander Verlag in 2002 as *Die Insel*) and David McKee's *The Conquerors* (Andersen Press, 2004) and *Tusk Tusk* (Andersen Press, 1978).

The Island offers a bleak view of mankind's propensity to be influenced by a lynch mob mentality. Here is a picturebook that provides a stark contrast to the 'pinky aesthetics' bemoaned by Wolf Erlbruch. Once again, we have to look to Australasia for an English-language edition (Allen & Unwin, Australia, 2007).

With limited use of colour and dark Honoré Daumier-like drawings, Greder creates an island world that is turned upside

Below and opposite: Armin Greder offers little in the way of hope in *The Island*. A dark, classical visual tone combines with a bleak view of mankind's ability to see 'aliens' as being to blame for society's ills.

So they took him in.

down by the arrival of a naked, wretched-looking man, washed up on the shore. What possible harm can this sorry figure cause? But gradually he becomes a focus of blame, a convenient scapegoat for all the islanders' ills, all their fears. Mothers use him as the bogeyman with which to threaten their children if they don't eat their food. *The Island* plots the gradual spread of suspicion and fear of someone different. It is a bleak book that doesn't offer any hope in the form of a traditional happy ending, but its universal message is powerfully conveyed.

In *The Conquerors* and *Tusk Tusk* David McKee takes a much gentler look at man's apparent perennial need to invade and conquer his neighbours' territories. McKee's approach is a more typical, less direct Anglo-Saxon one than Greder's, and uses humour and irony to tackle equally serious material. *The Conquerors* is a beautifully understated book that tells the tale of a small nation which, rather than engaging in war, prefers to devote its time to culture in the form of storytelling, singing songs and quietly celebrating its heritage. Its larger and aggressively expansionist neighbour, led by the stereotypical medal-strewn general, continually invades the nation but somehow never conquers it. The invading soldiers are greeted quietly, told stories and sung to; eventually they have such a good time that before they know it they themselves are being conquered with culture and charm. The book sends a profound message with effortless elegance.

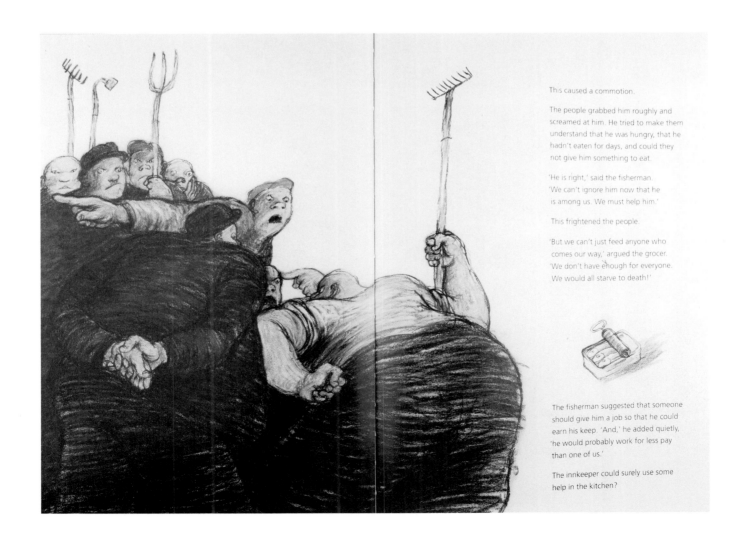

This caused a commotion.

The people grabbed him roughly and screamed at him. He tried to make them understand that he was hungry, that he hadn't eaten for days, and could they not give him something to eat.

'He is right,' said the fisherman. 'We can't ignore him now that he is among us. We must help him.'

This frightened the people.

'But we can't just feed anyone who comes our way,' argued the grocer. 'We don't have enough for everyone. We would all starve to death!'

The fisherman suggested that someone should give him a job so that he could earn his keep. 'And,' he added quietly, 'he would probably work for less pay than one of us.'

The innkeeper could surely use some help in the kitchen?

Although McKee's *Tusk Tusk* is a small picturebook that features apparently simple, sweet, stylized elephants set against a colourful jungle background, its themes are hatred, racism, war, violence, difference, outsiders. It is designed and marketed for a young audience, but McKee offers a no-holds-barred view of some of the worst aspects of humanity. The Eden-like existence of the elephants in a land bursting with gorgeous vegetation soon ends as the black elephants hate the white elephants and vice versa. Trunks turn into guns, and war and killing ensue until the environment is laid waste, and the peace-loving elephants are left no choice but to hide in the depths of the forest. Decades later, as the land once more bursts into beautiful life, grey elephants appear, the progeny of their peace-

loving forebears. The reader believes McKee will provide a happy ending after all, but the final sentence in the book is: 'But recently the little ears and the big ears have been giving each other strange looks.' McKee is not afraid to challenge children. He is better known for the gentler elephant series, *Elmer*, but it is worth pointing out that even here the hero is multicoloured and multicultural.

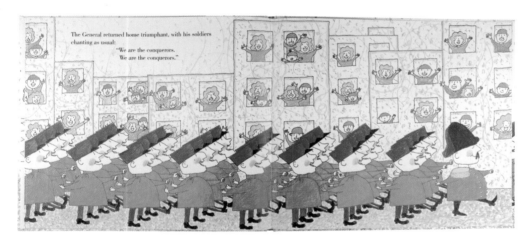

Left and below: In books such as *The Conquerors* and *Tusk Tusk*, David McKee's use of rich colour and a relatively traditional picturebook language belie the underlying seriousness of the messages that are conveyed.

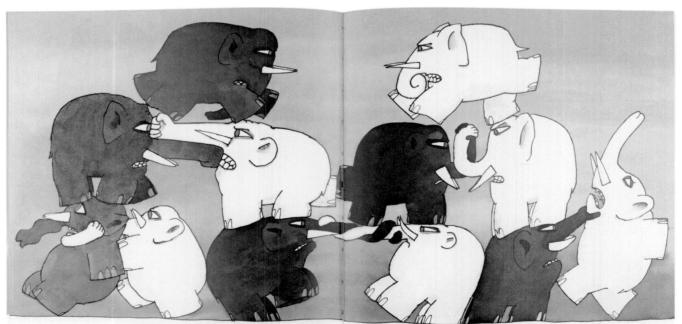

and on, and on...

Professional case study: Portraying physical love

Sabien Clement
Jij lievert

The issue of sex education for the young has long been a battleground, and will always provoke a wide range of views and standpoints. But the visual portrayal of physical love in a picturebook is a difficult and challenging task for any artist. In *Jij lievert* (De Eenhoorn, 2002, subsequently published as *Amourons-nous*), Sabien Clement demonstrates that it is possible to tackle the subject with sensitivity, humour and charm.

The book is a collaboration between Clement and writer Geert De Kockere, whose poems about love and being in love the artist interprets. In *Colouring Outside the Lines* (Flemish Literature Fund, 2006) Marita Vermeulen writes eloquently about Clement's illustrations:

The pen drawings and coloured shapes in Jij lievert represent human beings in all their vulnerability. The fragile lines can scarcely rein in the sensual bodies. Within the pictures there is

a constant friction between the physical and the emotional. It appears as though Clement's characters hardly have enough body and limbs to express their love and their anxiety. Arms and legs that are much too long or just too short touchingly symbolize the awkwardness of human beings trying to demonstrate their love.

It is Clement's nervous, searching line that gives the book a rare innocence and warmth. The pictures dance playfully in, out and around the text, sometimes expanding the words, sometimes offsetting them. As Vermeulen observes: 'When the text is explicit, her pictures are ambiguous; when the text is harsh, she adds gentleness.' Clement is always respectful to the spirit of the text.

Speaking about her approach to such a project, Clement makes clear the importance of understanding the author's intentions:

When a writer asks me to make illustrations for his book, first I read the text, but also I like to meet with the writer, to know his thinking, his opinions, his vision. I always ask about the age of the intended audience but when I start the work, I try not to let it rein me in too much. I just try to build an atmosphere that fits.

Asked about the tricky issue of defining suitability for children, she says:

Hmmm… that's very fragile. It even depends on the education of parents. A child of eight can sometimes be more grown-up than one of fourteen. I remember a girl of about eight looking at Amourons-nous. She wasn't shocked or embarrassed at all to see naked people. She acted very normally and liked it in a nice, gentle way. In my opinion, Amourons-nous isn't shocking at all. It's love described in a gentle, universal way. So in answer to the question, I would say that you cannot put in boxes what is or isn't suitable. Except when the subject is genuinely shocking.

On the broader subject of her sense of self as an artist/ illustrator, Clement says:

I see myself as a 'drawer from the heart'. If this becomes a picturebook, that's fine. If it becomes a painting, that's fine too. In my free time, I draw – just for myself – on a big canvas or in a small diary book. I do life drawing just because I adore it. I like to balance on the edge of being an illustrator and a painter/ creative artist. If a picturebook transcends the normal, if the pictures move you emotionally, then for me it's fine art. But I am not really concerned about the words.

Previous page and below: In *Jij lievert* (subsequently published as *Amourons-nous*), Sabien Clement's delicate drawings perfectly complement Geert De Kockere's text on the subject of love. Clement hits just the right tone of gentle humour without diminishing the seriousness of the subject.

Draai lief om,
zoek de betekenis op
en neem daarvan
het omgekeerde.

Zo is het
jou te hebben.

Ik was jou
aan het schrijven
en jij was mij
aan het lezen.

Maar lang duurde het niet.

Want ik was onleesbaar
en jij onbeschrijfelijk.

Student case study: Stylistic suitability

Rebecca Palmer and Kow Fong Lee

The following case study examines the nature of the stylistic suitability of pictorial imagery for children, through two masters students currently grappling with the concept.

As with all areas of creativity, individual stylistic identities and preoccupations vary greatly from one illustration student to another. Each of the two featured here have highly distinctive visual 'signatures' despite the fact that their work is still evolving and developing. Although studying in the same masters cohort, both work in very different visual idioms. Kow Fong works entirely in digital media to create his richly coloured artworks, while Palmer uses traditional media – pencil and oil paint (thinned with Liquin) – to produce her much more subdued, sombre-hued illustrations. Their respective approaches reflect and represent many aspects of their differing personal creative journeys, but each is aiming to 'speak' to the child through a personal voice.

Personality and, of course, cultural background play a large part in the development of these students' unique languages. Kow Fong is from Singapore, where graphic traditions tend to embrace the use of intense colours and highly stylized characterization. Palmer is British and has a keen interest in northern European narrative art. As with all students of children's book illustration, there is always something of a juggling act to

Below: Kow Fong Lee's illustrations are constructed digitally using a drawing tablet and digital colour.

What should I do?

be performed – retaining the integrity of one's own distinctive artistic voice, while endeavouring to ensure that this voice communicates effectively with a particular audience, or at least that it convinces publishers that it will do so.

Each of the two artists is conscious of these issues, but is concentrating primarily on creating work he/she feels to be true rather than allowing him/herself to second-guess audience needs. On the subject of whether her work might be perceived as suitable for children, Palmer says:

It's certainly something I have been thinking about. Agents have said that I need to 'lighten' it for children. But at the moment I feel these drawings get at the real people I am trying to portray. The challenge to make my drawing more 'appropriate', though, is one that I think is worth taking on.

I am exploring various media but don't want to lose the fundamental way in which I draw. I am interested in everyday life. Children notice these little things and I want to share them. I don't want a conscious style to interfere. As with drawing, the kind of writing I admire is the sort that acts as a seamless conduit for the message of observation and truth – no intrusive style. With words you have to read everything but with pictures you have options to interpret and take what you need.

Kow Fong says:

With regards to the importance of keeping a target audience-age in mind when making a picturebook, I think we can see it from two perspectives. As an illustrator, I'm not too mindful as to who I'm drawing for. I'm simply creating pictures to be

aesthetically pleasing and satisfying, that will touch the heart or arouse the interest, I hope, of any of my viewers. I believe the appreciation of visual art is universal, is beyond, and should not be confined by, the age of your audience. On the other hand, the composition of the text, or the way of the narration, would be more closely linked to your audience's capacity of acceptance. The choice of vocabulary, the standard of the language, the way of expressing a certain theme or idea of the story, would have to be catered to our intended primary reader. A picturebook does not serve the purpose of just telling a story. The illustrations in fact have a rather crucial role to perform: of enhancing one's aesthetical awareness.

On the subject of the suitability of digitally generated artwork for children's picturebooks, he says:

I'm not too sure if it is really a general sentiment among publishers to react negatively to digital aesthetic, some do definitely show preference for traditionally rendered illustrations over digital art. They do have their reasons and I respect that. The versatility of digital tools has opened up new possibilities for illustrators, in achieving certain visual effect more conveniently and working more effectively. To me, working digitally is simply a change of tool. I'm still doing hand-rendered drawings but with a tablet and illustrating software instead of paper and colouring material. I don't see digital illustration as just a fad. It is here to stay. With more illustrators going digital, we can expect to see more diverse digital artworks in styles and aesthetic possibilities. The world will learn to appreciate digital art, it is just a matter of time.

Left, below and opposite: Rebecca Palmer's work is generated entirely through traditional media, using subdued colour and hand-rendered lettering.

Below: Only the very first storyboard drawings are rendered on paper in Kow Fong Lee's working process.

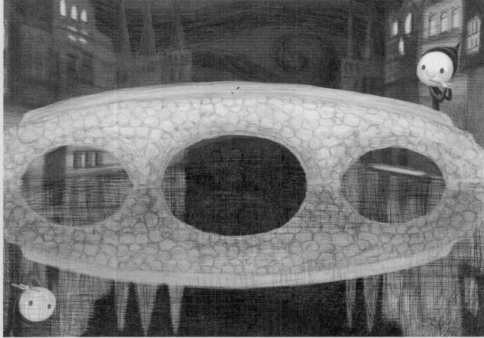

Could there be
someone
waiting at the
end
to hear my
stories?

He wonders.

PRINT AND PROCESS: THE SHOCK OF THE OLD

Left and below: Print Room: The various printmaking processes that were originally developed as a means of multiple reproduction have experienced a resurgence in popularity in recent years. Drawing (below) by Hannah Webb.

Opposite: To keep costs down, many books in the 1950s and 1960s were illustrated in two or three colours, which the artist rendered as separations, as in Helen Borten's illustrations to *Rain and Hail* by Franklyn M. Branley (Thomas Crowell, 1963). Many artists now choose to impose such limitations, despite the technology available.

The various processes and techniques that have been employed in book illustration during its evolution as an art form have, until very recently, been closely connected to the printing processes used to reproduce them. Artists have needed to be aware of the characteristics and limitations of reprographic technologies as they have developed their working methods. In the early days of printing, from the sixteenth through to the eighteenth century, the method of reproduction was in itself the artist's medium. The distinction we now make between the terms 'printing' and 'printmaking' did not exist. The artist carved an image on to a woodblock that was inked and printed repeatedly on to paper. A century or two later a skilled craftsman might be employed to translate an artist's image into a printable engraving. But with developments in technology, and later the arrival of the digital revolution towards the end of the twentieth century, it became clear that pretty much any medium could be reproduced satisfactorily. Highly sensitive laser scanners could 'see' and separate colours and textures with great accuracy. Then Photoshop and other software appeared and for a while seemed to suggest that the paper and pencil were becoming redundant. Suddenly it could all be done on screen and sent to the commissioner at the touch of a button. It was no longer necessary to tear up pictures because the colour had gone wrong; it was possible to erase and fiddle indefinitely.

For a while, infatuation with software meant the Photoshop aesthetic dominated. Many designers decided they were now illustrators. The ability to move found material around, to appropriate and import any kind of image, briefly blinded many to the importance of the basics of drawing and thinking. With any new technology, predictions tend, with the benefit of hindsight, to say more about the time in which they are made than the time they purport to predict. Happily, the handmade mark has refused to go away. That direct line of contact between brain, hand and paper still has a magical power. Picturebooks

today continue to display the use of a wide variety of traditional media – pencil, inks, watercolour, oils, acrylics and so on. But there is a particularly noticeable revival in the use of printmaking processes for creating artwork for illustration. Despite the speed with which imagery can be generated on screen, the time-consuming methods and raw effects of ancient relief processes, such as wood- and linocut, have made a major comeback in the early twenty-first century. To some extent this may simply be a natural, cyclical reaction against what is seen as a rather cold digital aesthetic. However, it is now possible to generate imagery that begins with hands-on methods but which can then be manipulated and controlled with greater freedom using digital software. It is probably fair to say that the overwhelming majority of artists under the age of 40 working in the picturebook field today use digital media to some extent, if only as a cleaning-up tool. Alongside this, and with the ongoing development of the screen-based E-picturebook, ever greater attention is paid to the physical form of the picturebook. The choice of papers, coverboards and print effects such as spot lamination, embossing and laser cutting have become important aspects of the development of the book as these assert its physical, sensual identity as distinct from its identity on the screen.

For the artist, there are many attractions in using the various printmaking processes. While these have traditionally been seen as a way of creating limited editions of signed prints, to augment sales of one-off paintings or artefacts, they can also play an important role in the development of an individual artist's visual language. Placing a technical process between artist and paper introduces an element of accident and surprise to the outcome. This lessening of control frequently has the by-product of lessening self-consciousness in mark-making.

The following are brief definitions of the most commonly used printmaking processes.

The water vapor is carried by the air.
When the wind blows, the water vapor moves.
The air blows one way and then another.
The air goes down and it goes up.
The air goes up and away from the earth.

16   17

Relief printing

The act of cutting away at a surface, usually wood, linoleum or vinyl, in order to leave a raised area that can be rolled with ink and pressed against paper to leave a reverse impression of the image, is known as relief printing.

One of the techniques used to create the raised area is engraving, which made a comeback in the first half of the twentieth century with artists such as Claire Leighton and Gwen Raverat, whose work demonstrated that it could still find a place in book illustration. Wood engraving, as distinct from woodcutting, is a process of cutting into the dense end grain (the surface made when slicing through the trunk) of a hardwood such as box or lemon. Today, it is used mainly in the world of finely printed books from private presses; a few artists, such as John Lawrence and Christopher Wormell, keep the tradition alive in the mainstream. However, both Lawrence and Wormell engrave more often on vinyl or lino.

Woodcutting is distinguished from wood engraving by the way the wood is cut – along the grain or 'plank' of a softwood,

Below: John Lawrence's illustrations to Robert Louis Stevenson's *Treasure Island* (Walker Books, 2009) are created by engraving on vinyl floor tiles. Each colour is printed separately and then cut and collaged.

which gives a raw and textured finish. Since Antonio Frasconi repopularized its use in the 1950s (see pp. 29–30) it has remained an occasional medium for the picturebook. A notable current exponent is the Belgian artist Isabelle Vandenabeele. Vandenabeele carves wood in the traditional way, to leave a raised image surface to be inked, but initially prints all the colour separations in black so that they can be scanned and the colours added in Photoshop. This retains all the textures of the crude print process but gives the artist far greater control over colour.

The linocut seems to be currently more popular than ever, with artists all over the world enjoying its unique textures and effects. It was perhaps Edward Bawden (see pp. 23–24) who first popularized this apparently crude process by bringing his unique wit and orderly sense of design to bear upon its use, thereby propelling what had been seen as a 'kitchen table' process into the world of fine art and design.

Card printing is another process that is also showing signs of a comeback. This is a simple process of cutting away at layered cardboard to leave a raised image area that gives pleasing organic textures when printed.

Separating colours for the various forms of relief printing means using methods to ensure that when the different ones are printed on top of each other they are correctly registered, and thereby make visual sense. But the inevitable misregistrations that occur during the process can be aesthetically appealing, and have often been seized upon by artists and incorporated playfully into their work. The British artist John Minton once described his own working method as 'the successful steering of accident'.[1]

---

[1] Michael Rothenstein, *Looking at Paintings*. George Routledge & Sons, 1947.

Below left: The English artist, Edward Bawden, elevated the linocut to a more respectable position as a medium for making art and illustration. Here, in *The Sixpence that Rolled Away* by Louis MacNeice (Faber, 1956), his original linocut prints are translated into metal line blocks in order to print on a larger commercial scale than the original lino could survive.

Below right: Card printing is one of the more rustic media that is making a comeback. Layers of coarse card are cut into with a knife, leaving a raised image area to be inked and printed, as in this print by Chloë Cheese.

Opposite: Pieter van Ouheusden and Kevin Vanwontrghem's *Liefde kan niet zonder Liefde*.

Below and bottom left: Colour woodcuts by Isabelle Vandenabeele from Geert De Kockere's *Vorspel Van Een Gebroken Liefde* (De Eenhoorn, 2007).

Bottom right: Isabelle Vandenabeele at the 'Colouring Outside the Lines' exhibition at Cambridge School of Art.

Below: Kazuno Kohara's *The Haunted House* (Walker Books, 2008) was developed as a student project at Cambridge School of Art. The images are created as single colour linocuts, printed in black ink on orange paper with occasional use of collaged white tissue paper for the ghosts.

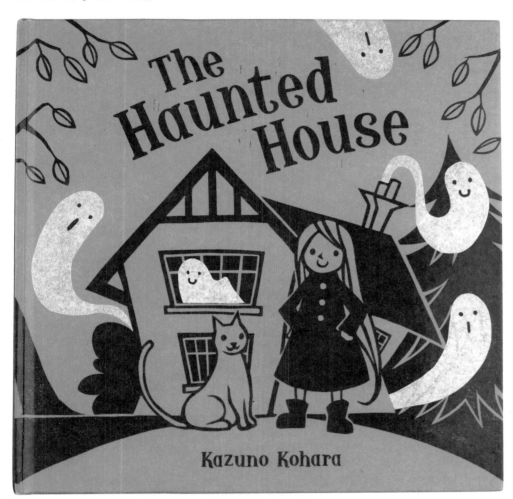

Below: Andrew Kulman's linocuts for *Red Light, Green Light* (ABC, 1992) feature strong shapes, limited colour and heavily-inked cuts that give texture and movement to the page.

Screen-printing

Screen-printing is not a process that is normally thought of as being appropriate for children's books. As a method of reproduction it may have its origins in Japanese stencilling, but it came into its own in the early twentieth century as a means of printing on a large scale. It was especially suitable for flags and posters. The process is similar to stencilling: an ink-resistant substance is used to paint negative images on a screen – for many years silk was stretched tightly across a frame – and a squeegee is dragged across its surface to force a thin film of ink through the unpainted areas to create positive images. A different screen is made for each of the colours that will be printed. The inks used can be mixed with a medium that allows for varying levels of transparency so that layers of colour can be overlaid to create new ones. Although most picturebook artists choose Photoshop to create such effects, the process of screen-printing is by far the best way to learn about the subtleties of colour layering.

Below: In her *Chain of Happiness* illustration, Marta Altés screen-prints with three colours.

Etching/intaglio

Like relief printing, etching, also known as intaglio, involves cutting or engraving a surface – in this case a metal plate, most commonly copper or zinc. The difference is that the engraved marks, rather than the area around them, carry the ink that is to be printed on the paper. The plate is usually coated with an acid-resistant substance through which lines are drawn with an etching tool. The plate is then placed in an acid bath for a period of time so that the lines are 'bitten' more deeply. The longer the plate is left in the acid, the more robust the line. Ink is rubbed into the plate then wiped off its surface, leaving ink in the bitten lines. Damp paper is laid on the plate, which is passed through a press, leaving a reverse impression.

Textures and tones can be created through a process known as aquatinting. This involves placing a layer of resin or sugar on the plate; the acid bites around the finely granulated texture. Different gradations can be achieved, depending once again on how long the plate is exposed to the acid. Such an apparently complex process seems unsuitable for making picturebooks but an increasing number of examples have appeared in recent years.

Below: Kaatje Vermeire's complex etchings are delicately coloured.

Opposite: Kaatje Vermeire's etching process helps to give a unified overall mood to her books.

Right and below: *The Little Red Fish* by Tae-Eun Yoo (Dial, 2007) is illustrated with sepia-printed etchings with sparing use of subtle shades of warmer colour.

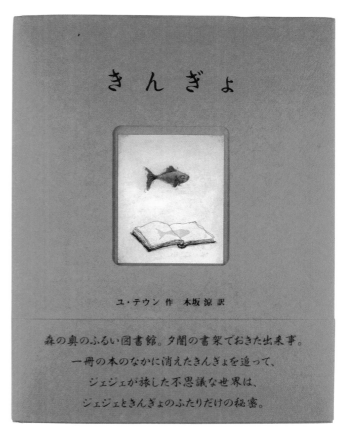

きんぎょ

ユ・テウン 作　木坂 涼 訳

森の奥のふるい図書館。夕闇の書架でおきた出来事。
一冊の本のなかに消えたきんぎょを追って、
ジェジェが旅した不思議な世界は、
ジェジェときんぎょのふたりだけの秘密。

Lithography

Lithography was invented by Aloysius Senefelder in Germany in the late eighteenth century, and is the ancestor of modern commercial printing methods. The process exploits the mutual antipathy of oil and water, which allows an image to be transferred from a smooth surface, originally limestone but today a metal plate, commonly zinc, to paper. The image can be drawn on to the surface with a greasy, water-resistant crayon or ink. When printing ink is applied it sticks to the drawn area but washes away from the rest of the surface, leaving a slightly raised, inked image that will transfer to paper when the plate goes through a press. As with other print processes, multiple colours can be overlaid in registration. Once again, the image is printed in reverse. Commercial lithography is known as offset lithography as vast self-inking machines transfer the reverse image on to a rubber blanket, then on to the paper, and it is consequently the right way round.

Right and below: *Red Striped Pants*, originally published by Borim Press in South Korea, was created using direct lithography. The lithographic prints were scanned and reproduced without any further digital intervention by the artist, who has worked primarily in the fields of ceramic and gallery installation work.

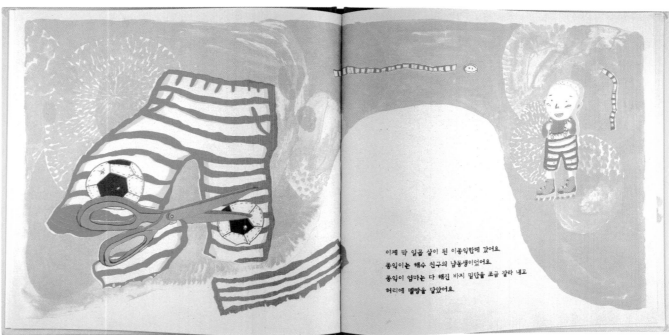

Monotype and monoprint

Monotype and monoprint describe a process that is essentially a way of transferring an image to paper, rather like making a printed painting or drawing. It is essentially used for a one-off print, though in theory the difference between the two terms is that a monoprint can allow for more than one print of the same image. However, the images will never be identical. Monoprints can be made in various ways. One is to paint an image on to a surface and transfer it to paper, in a press or by hand pressure. Another method is to lay down a surface of ink on glass, then lay paper over it and draw on the paper, thereby pressing through the paper on to the ink; this leaves a reverse impression of the drawing on the other side of the paper, along with random textures picked up around it. Any form of monoprinting embraces a greater degree of unpredictability and accident than most other processes.

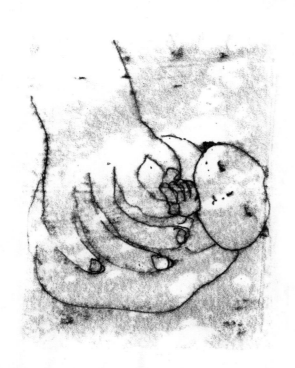

I have wrapped you up with all my love, and have laid my hand on you.

Right: Susan Chin's monoprint shows the diffused line and random background texture that characterize the process.

Below: Nicola Killen's *Not Me!* (Egmont, 2010) was developed as a student project at Cambridge School of Art. She used a range of 'table-top' print processes – monoprint, hand-cut rubber stamps and anything that came to hand.

Digital
printmaking

As so many artists confirm, the computer's role is most
commonly to bring together and assemble a range of other
media. Imagery is sometimes still created entirely through
particular software such as Photoshop and Illustrator. But the
arrival of the eBook in its various forms heralds a new stage
in the history of print and the picturebook, which is looked
at in more detail in chapter 7.

Right: Mike Smith's illustrations
for his award-winning student project,
Edward Hopper and the Carrot Crunch,
were created by generating the line-
drawing and the colour elements
separately and then reassembling them
digitally. This is a method that echoes
that of Edward Ardizzone (see p. 21)
some 80 years previously.

Professional case study: The handmade picturebook

Liz Loveless

The particular effects that screen-printing traditionally creates (flat colour with areas of transparent overlay creating further colours) are usually replicated these days by using Photoshop. But Liz Loveless is an artist who uses screen-printing both as technique and a method of reproduction for self-publishing. Loveless creates hand-printed books in limited editions for children and adults, each one signed and numbered. Like many illustrators, she was initially unsure which area of art and design practice to study. Her interest in pattern and surface led her to take a first degree in textile design. There has always been a close relationship between this and illustration, and the process of screen-printing perhaps binds the two together. Loveless explains how she moved to book-making:

There was a great deal of colour theory on the textiles course and the market was dominated by floral designs. I think I drove my tutor mad by wanting to be figurative and narrative. I was also influenced by Russian graphic traditions. I had left school at 16 without A levels and had worked as a pattern cutter for French Connection. After the textiles degree I took an MA in illustration at Camberwell College of Art, where I was greatly encouraged in the direction of children's books by Janet Wooley. After completing the course I worked as a freelance illustrator doing editorial work and used screen-printing on some commercially published picturebooks. But I was never entirely happy with them. It was my husband who suggested that I 'do my own'.

Loveless took a bookbinding course in order to better understand the physical make-up of books, but used a commercial bookbinder for her editions, making 350 books

Below and overleaf: The hand-printed, limited-edition books of Liz Loveless have proved to be a viable and affordable alternative to the products of mainstream publishing.

Stop looking at those **CAMERIERI**
and the washing on the line,
go to Giacomo's favourite restaurant
and have **GELATI** cherry pie!

in the first instance and going up to 650 for later titles. Clearly, the question of how to sell the books was, and still is, a key issue. As she explains, it has been a case of gradually building up a network of outlets:

The first place to stock my books was a lovely little shop in east London (Shelf, in Cheshire Street). I was in the shop, browsing, and told the owners about my books. They invited me to bring them in. I started in a modest way. I sent one to the Museum of Childhood and they asked me to send it to the main Victoria and Albert collection. The Tate Gallery also took one. I sell in other, smaller galleries such as St. Jude's in Norfolk. It's mostly 'word of mouth' really.

Loveless sees the self-published, limited-edition, handmade book as something of an antidote to the mass-market children's publishing industry. Having experienced both of these worlds, she feels that the small-scale private press gives her far greater artistic and editorial freedom, and also allows her to sell the books over a longer period of time compared to the short shelf-life of many commercially published books:

I am not a particularly commercially astute person, and I know that if I pushed harder in this direction I could be a lot more successful. But I have already made more money from each handmade book than I did from the commercially published ones, albeit over a period of five years or so. There is no bureaucracy and there are no editorial restrictions, a privilege only reserved for the highly successful authors in commercial publishing.

Ironically, Loveless has discovered that it is actually more lucrative to sell editions of individual prints than entire books, as people seem willing to spend as much on a mounted print as on a bound book. But she continues to create new picturebooks that are original works of art as well as practical, affordable, functioning children's picturebooks.

Professional case study: Merging old and new technologies

Claudia Boldt

Originally from Cologne in Germany, Claudia Boldt took an MA in illustration at Kingston University in Britain after previously studying at the Glasgow School of Art in Scotland. Her work has been selected for the prestigious Bologna Illustration Exhibition and catalogue. Boldt's first book, *Queens, Astronauts and Extraordinary Sausages*, is published by Childsplay. Her working method, like that of many young artists now, involves integrating a range of media and approaches, traditional and digital. Speaking about her working methods she explains:

Once the layout works in pencil I cut out stencils from Scratch-Foam. It is a thin foam made for children to use instead of linocut. I use it to imitate what I liked about screen-printing! It is much easier to cut and handle, although it is a little more difficult to make good prints in terms of flat, even colour. Moreover, the stencils can often only be used a few times as they can easily be damaged in the press. The press is a hand letterpress which can also be used for block printing. But

Below: Some of the various stages of Claudia Boldt's 'kitchen table' processes are shown here – a Scratch-Foam print is made in black before the image is coloured digitally; the foam is cut into shape and hand-pressed with ink, spreader and roller.

recently I have just been using hand rollers and no press any more. Printing with the hand letterpress or a roller in my studio is cheaper and quicker than using a commercial print studio!

Moreover, using stencils has the advantage that the process of building up the image is more flexible in terms of reworking parts of the illustration.

The prints are scanned in and coloured. The colour is applied with the computer to save time. I would often add details with line drawings. I use a mix of pens, pencils and ink, and again scan the originals and add them on another layer in Photoshop.

Below and opposite: *Stargazers, Skyscrapers and Extraordinary Sausages* by Claudia Boldt reflects contemporary trends in combining the handmade and the digital.

Professional case study: From screen to screen

Gwénola Carrère
ABC des Petites Annonces

ABC des Petites Annonces (Topipittori, 2008) by the Belgian artist Gwénola Carrère is a picturebook that feels visually, stylistically fresh yet at the same time harks back to earlier forms of printing. Carrère's distinctive digital graphic language did not evolve randomly. It grew from a background solidly based in printmaking, in particular screen-printing, and these origins can be clearly traced in the idioms that she employs. Carrère's work is redolent of Russian traditions in book illustration and of the *pochoir* techniques that were in vogue in the 1920s and 1930s (see p. 19). *Pochoir* was a method of hand-colouring illustrations in books by applying watercolour or gouache through specially made metal stencils.

When asked about the connections between old screen and new screen, Carrère says:

Yes, my visual identity found its real consistency the day I started screen-printing. Before that, I was much into painting, but I was very rarely satisfied. When I started to scan my paintings to screen-print them, I realized I had reached a whole

This page and opposite: Gwénola Carrère's *ABC* uses digital media to create a retro aesthetic that echoes the effects of stencil-based print processes of the early twentieth century.

new and so exciting visual world. The limitations of the screen-printing technique gave me an amazing new sense of freedom (how ironic, isn't it!). As for the Russian, 'retro' element – well yes, but not directly. I mean, the day I discovered the golden age of Russian illustration (1920–30) was a big day, but it was a few years before ABC. So of course I had Russian art in mind while doing ABC, for the shapes mostly (a sort of 'essential' feeling) but there was also another, maybe more vivid challenge for me in this book: trying to find the atmosphere I loved so much in my so old children's books. So I thought about these picturebooks from the fifties, published by Père Castor and Les Deux Coqs d'Or. And also, I thought a lot about Richard Scarry. So I had these references in mind. But the challenge was to not go and look at these books for real. Just let the memories speak…

Carrère has combined working as a printmaker, artists' book-maker and teacher with her work in mainstream publishing. She initially produced a handmade artist's book for children:

It took me almost two years to make this first book (it was in 2002 to 2003). Because before that, I had no style, I was a real 'chameleon'. So the whole challenge of this book was to find a harmony, something that would make me want to stop being a chameleon, but at the same time, something open enough to make me feel unlimited…

The story came to me while playing with figures I cut out of reproductions of classic paintings from the museum of Vienna (I grew up in Vienna). I found a character made out of these different pieces: a head, a back, one perfect leg and two arms. But I just couldn't find the missing leg. That was the start of the story…

The images are constructed entirely in Photoshop. As Carrère explains:

Nobody believes it, but I use Photoshop every day. Even for typography. For me it's the best way to combine scanned things and digital things (digital things are for instance typography, drawn or typed).

Student case study:
Experimental narrative sequence in monotype

Yann Kebbi

Yann Kebbi is a student studying at the Design Department of Hamburg University of Applied Sciences. His series of monotype prints was selected by the jury for the prestigious Bologna Illustration Exhibition in 2010. The prints have a fluid, painterly quality typical of the effects of this medium but also retain a highly individual, personal narrative language. Kebbi says about his working process:

Each of the monotypes was made in several printings on the same paper, like the principle of silkscreen printing. The surface can be whatever you like since you just paint on it but it must fit into the press. Copper, zinc, plastic – I used zinc. The inks I use are either for etching or lithography, offset inks. In fact any inks which are washable with alcohol, or white spirit, so it doesn't get dry too fast, and most of all you can come back on it, erase and start again, etc.

The interest of the monotype is that even if it's supposed to be printed only once, there is still what could be called a 'ghost' of the previous picture on the plate, so you can print it again or play with it.

For the pictures I first print the black areas. With a roller I fully cover the plate of black ink (used for etching, it's called encre vignette in France, the softer the ink, the better) and then with some cloth I take off the black to keep only the areas I want, then I print. This step allows me to have a full and deep black, and also to give depth even to the areas supposed to be white on the picture.

Then I use the coloured inks and alcohol, and I paint on the plate and make as many printings as I need for the picture to be complete. Like I said you have a 'ghost' of the previous picture on the plate, so you always see (more or less) what you are painting on, and where it's going to be on the picture. It's the same process of thinking as silkscreen printing, but it's more about drawing and accidents.

The set of images was created in response to the Bologna competition brief which required five images from a continuous sequence. So, in a sense, the series is a wordless pictorial sequence from an imaginary potential picturebook.

The images are related to a picture I had in mind, because of a dream, so it's not related to a text. In this picture everything was in double, so I had the idea of that one man, who wouldn't visually fit in with the usual aspects of life, since he is different and has no double.

Besides, I wanted to explore the technique of monotype and create a solid series of pictures, and the idea of the double went well with the fact that in monotype you can reprint and it creates like an echo. So it's less about a story than a graphic principle really.

For me, it was a challenge to create pictures with this technique, pictures that can be attractive and understandable for the young ones. Since I didn't start from a text there isn't a real story, but I related the pictures to different views of different situations of communal urban life; the picture's order is like a trail. So basically there isn't any real end yet, only a trail and the demonstration in different places of this man's loneliness.

Left: The fluid effects of ink being wiped and moved around on a smooth surface are evident in Yann Kebbi's monotype prints.

Professional case study: Digital printmaking

Fabian Negrin
On va au parc!

Fabian Negrin is an artist whose work is familiar in many European countries but who is always experimenting with new techniques and methods. So much so that his work is often unrecognizable from one book to the next. As well as using a wide range of traditional media, he has experimented with various stylistic and structural methods in making picturebooks. In 2010 he was awarded the Bologna Ragazzi prize for non-fiction for *The Riverbank* (published by The Creative Company). In *On va au parc!* (Rouergue, 2009) Negrin tells the story of a small boy imploring his father to take him to the park. The boy's pleading becomes increasingly desperate and increasingly loud as his father sleeps from page to page. The 'noise' of the attempts to waken the father from his slumber is often represented typographically.

For this picturebook Negrin used a form of digital printmaking – creating separate colours as flat ink-and-wash 'stencils' then scanning and colouring in Photoshop. The white of the paper

Right and opposite: In *On va au parc!* Fabian Negrin uses the computer to assemble flat colour separations that begin life as inked shapes on paper. The shapes are scanned and then coloured and overlaid in Photoshop.

is frequently used to create negative shapes. Colours are kept entirely flat but with occasional washy textures and transparency allowing for overprinting to make extra colour. Here the computer is used, as so often nowadays, to create an effect that looks as 'undigital' as possible. In fact, the book is inspired by early twentieth-century Russian design and printing but, as Negrin explains, the typography has varied according to the publishers in different countries:

The illustrations were built through ink lines and spots on paper that I scanned, put together and coloured with Photoshop. I looked for a 'style' that would be reminiscent of the work of Levedev, Lapsin and other Russian illustrators of children's books that I really love. In the Italian version of the book my typographic design, more rigorous, was left unaltered. In the French version there were some changes, and the introduction of fonts less obviously taken from the Russian golden age of children's books, but these changes meet in fact the 'noisiness' that is characteristic

of the story, which made me accept the changes introduced by Rouergue's art director.

Negrin is unusual among illustrators in the way that he has no distinctive stylistic identity or preferred medium. But he has strong views on this:

The stylistic changes that one can find in my several books are due, in part, to my personality: I love trying new techniques and styles, while I get bored doing always the same thing. On the other hand, though, I think that this is the only way to make illustrations really meet a text and become one with it, in children's books. People using only one style limit themselves to reproduce the same forms over and over, independently from the tone of a story. The same forms for a horror tale or a love story, for a fairy tale and a science fiction one, without the least shift in the register and atmosphere. I think that very often this way of illustrating does not work. To attach predefined

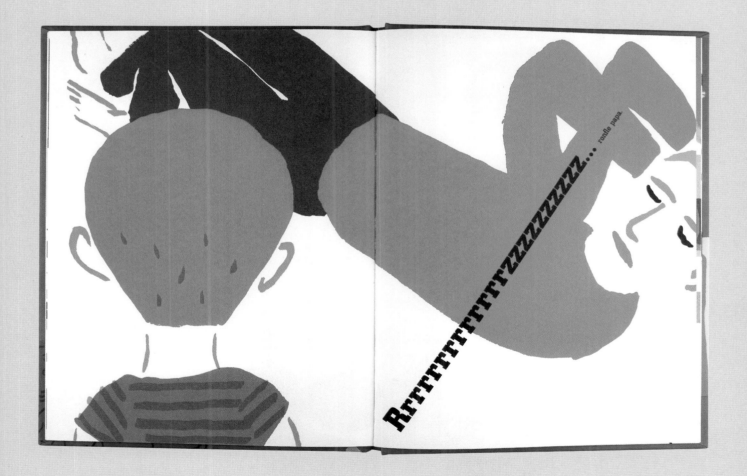

forms to any story makes the forms themselves less meaningful, it makes them become some sort of decoration, where the drawings live a life of their own without really biting the text. I am not the only one to work in this way. Without in any way wishing to compare my work to theirs, Maurice Sendak writes more or less the same things somewhere in Caldecott & Co, *Milton Glaser says the same in* Art is Work, *Art Spiegelman does not look for a stylistic consistency in his various works and sometimes within the same one, the books by Igram Ibatouline are very different from one another. So are the ones by Levedev, and not even Rackham had only one way of working. I am not in a bad company, after all, am I?*

Views on this subject will, of course, vary and most artists will feel they have little choice in the matter – their so-called 'style' is an involuntary, unconscious identity that cannot be discarded whether it is desirable or not. Ultimately, it is content that should dictate method, as Negrin continues:

To me to work at a children's book is the most serious thing one could do, but also the most exciting one, the one in which I can throw all of my self and of my skills, keeping in touch with the world around. In the first place, as an illustrator, what connects my work as a whole is the total devotion to the story I am illustrating. This happens always, even when the economic aspect does not justify it. Secondly, it is the starting point in my work – when I begin a new book and consider different possible types of images until I find a certain visual world that is perfect for the words – that is always the same. That moment, when I search for an illustrative style that is in tune with the literary style of a certain story, is, I think, the most important one of my work. Even when one compares two of my books that seem to have been done by two different people, there will always be this same initial intention, a search for a unity between text and image. Of course this relationship between text and images must not be a simple one: it can be ironic, parallel, contradictory, quarrelsome; we can also say, through the images, the opposite of what the words are saying. But it must be a choice, and it does not have to be so only because our style is of a certain kind and we cannot draw in any other way.

THE CHILDREN'S PUBLISHING INDUSTRY

Above: *It's a Book* by Lane Smith

Children's book publishing is a massive global industry, one that plays a significant role in the economies of many countries, particularly when successful books are exported as co-editions in other languages. For many smaller nations with minority languages, the traffic is predominantly in the other direction with well-known titles being imported and published in translation. But the picturebook also has a cultural role to play. Many of the smaller nations, such as Norway, Belgium and South Korea, value the indigenous book as part of their particular cultural and artistic heritage, and some provide subsidies to ensure that books that reflect this are published. Generally speaking, though, children's publishing is a commercial industry that involves writers, artists, designers, publishers, printers, marketing people and booksellers. These exist in an interdependent chain in an increasingly global context.

Around the world publishers can have very different ideas about picturebooks for children, but they also vary greatly within individual countries in the kind of books they publish. It is essential, therefore, that young artists and authors research carefully before approaching a publisher, to make sure they are fully acquainted with any particular visual 'flavour' of an individual publishing house.

For the aspiring picturebook maker, the publishing industry may seem intimidatingly large and confusing. Breaking into it is not easy. As with the world of writing, just getting your creation seen is the first hurdle. The economic climate of recent years has had a particular impact on the picturebook, with well-established authors and titles tending to dominate the market, often with seemingly endless versions of the same story or character. In countries with a free-market approach to commerce, selling books in supermarkets is having a major impact. These dominant chains often sell only a narrow range of picturebook titles, but with so many outlets this greatly affects sales. Publishers are eager to find new talent, however, so persistence is essential.

In this chapter we look at a range of publishing houses, large and small, hear different opinions from those who commission picturebooks, and examine how picturebooks come into being, and are marketed and sold. A series of case studies reveals the differing philosophies of publishing houses and more about the mechanics of getting picturebooks into shops and into the hands of the consumer.

Publishing houses

In a large, well-known publishing house, there may be an array of individuals in various posts who are responsible for commissioning new work: senior designers, commissioning editors, etc. In a small, independent publishing house there may be one or two individuals who are responsible for the whole process of design, editing, print management and distribution. The larger houses dominate the market but, as the case studies show, many small independent ones survive and flourish. Mergers and takeovers are common and it is sometimes difficult to know which company belongs to which as smaller companies are taken over but retain their name as an imprint within a larger one.

Below: Oliver Jeffers' first book, *How to Catch a Star*, was presented as a well-produced dummy to a selection of publishers who the author carefully researched beforehand.

The publishing process

Above: The graduation exhibition is still an important event for student picturebook makers. Most children's editors and designers at publishing houses make a point of scouring shows for new talent.

Approaching a publisher

The publishing process begins when the picturebook maker manages to make contact with the picturebook publisher. With most successful picturebooks now 'composed' by one person, the most common way to present an idea to a publisher is in the form of a dummy version of the proposed book. This is a mock-up of the whole book, and most commonly contains a few spreads that reproduce finished artwork with the remaining images in the form of rough pencil sketches. The text is included on each page. This allows a publisher to get a good feel for the overall structure of the book, the characterization, the pace and flow, the page-turning experience. There are a number of online companies who will create a one-off bound book relatively cheaply by uploading page designs on to a template. Some publishers are happy to receive PDFs by email but may well ask to see a dummy as well if the book interests them. If a picturebook idea is taken forward by a publisher, it is always likely that the editorial team will want to have an input on various aspects of the content, including the design, so there is little point in completing a book at this stage. The level of difficulty in actually getting your work seen, getting past the notorious 'slush pile', varies from one publisher to another. But most will try very hard to look at everything that comes their way.

The highly successful picturebook maker Oliver Jeffers might be seen as a model example of how to approach publishers on first leaving college. He struck a deal with a local printer to produce an edition of printed, bound dummies of what was to become his first book, *How to Catch a Star* (HarperCollins, 2004), in return for some original artworks. After researching the publishers whom he felt might be most sympathetic to his particular visual and conceptual approach, he mailed dummies to a group of carefully targeted 'top ten' editors. 'I sent the packages out on Tuesday and on Wednesday I received a call from Sue Buswell, publishing director for picturebooks at HarperCollins.'[1] So began an ongoing partnership. It's not usually quite that straightforward, but Jeffers' story does illustrate the importance of an organized and confident approach to selling an idea.

The larger the publishing house, the longer the chain of people and departments that need to be consulted and convinced before a book can go to contract. An editor sometimes has to wait for a prearranged acquisitions meeting at which to present a recently received picturebook proposal, and this can occasionally mean losing out to another publisher which is able to be quicker off the mark. Just occasionally, a new talent emerging at a graduation show attracts the interest of a number of publishers and causes a bidding war. The lucky object of the competition is then able to pick which publisher to go with, and money is not necessarily the only consideration. A mutually comfortable feeling about working together is very important.

[1] In conversation with Martin Salisbury at the British Association of Illustrators, March 2010.

The literary agent

Another way in which a publisher might be approached, or a publisher might approach an artist, is via a literary agent. The role of an agent is to represent and promote an individual, helping to maximize their earning power by making sure that what he or she does or produces is brought to the attention of as many potential sources of income as possible. Sportsmen and sportswomen, actors, writers and illustrators may choose to be represented by agencies. For providing this service, the agent will take a percentage of the income generated. Many illustrators choose not to be represented by an agent, while others are represented by artists' agents who seek work for their clients in a wide range of areas. Picturebook makers often prefer to be represented by literary agents who specialize in representing writers and artists who work mainly in publishing.

Penny Holroyde is an agent with the renowned Caroline Sheldon Literary Agency in London. She explains what she perceives to be the benefits for an artist of being represented by a literary agent: 'We charge substantially less than artists' agents –15 per cent as compared to anything up to 35 per cent. The main advantage to the artist is simply the greater exposure. The work is constantly being shown and we have an online presence too. We deal with all of the nuts and bolts, for example dealing with contracts, deadlines and hold-ups. Children's publishing is quite an idiosyncratic business. With our experience of the whole process we are able to say to the artist "This situation is perfectly normal" or "This is not normal".'

Day-to-day activities may involve meeting with publishers who are looking to match texts with suitable artists. On the other hand, publishers sometimes give picturebook deals to artists before they have suitable, publishable texts. In this situation, they speak to agents, looking for writers. Agents also attend the major book fairs, where they meet with publishers from many countries in the hope of securing deals. Literary agencies, like publishers, come in different sizes, but most strive to achieve a close working relationship with all their artists and writers.

Contracts and fees

A picturebook maker usually receives payment in the form of an advance and a royalty in the form of a percentage of the income on sales. Fees and contracts vary greatly from one country to another and from one publisher to another within any country. In many European and Far Eastern countries typical advances are considerably lower than those paid in Britain and the United States, but royalty percentages can be higher. The latter is often the case with smaller independent publishers, who are more likely than the bigger houses to take a risk on publishing an unknown author but may be less likely to be in a position to pay up front. Where the writer and illustrator of a picturebook are not the same person, the total of the two fees tends be higher than the fee paid to a single artist–author.

The initial payment for a book is usually in the form of an advance against royalties. This is paid before publication, and is often broken down into two or three payments, the first on signing of contract, the second on delivery of roughs, etc. A publisher may offer a two-book deal. The amount of the advance payment will, of course, depend on how many copies of a book the publisher expects to sell. A well-established picturebook maker with a strong record of sales will expect to receive a much higher advance than a first-time author. Royalties are only paid when the book has sold enough copies to pay off the advance. For most books, this actually never happens and in this eventuality the author is not expected to repay the advance.

A typical picturebook contract states the amount of the advance and the breakdown of payments. It includes detailed clauses on royalty payments on books sold at discount and on co-editions sold to other countries in translation. It is important to remember that the contract is not a 'sign it or forget it' arrangement. Publishers will be open to negotiation about the details. Most countries have a society of authors or a similar association, and membership of these can be very useful when it comes to contracts. A member can get help from an expert who will check over the contract and offer advice.

The editorial process

Once a contract has been signed, and deadlines agreed, the process of creating a book begins. With picturebooks the contract is often awarded on the basis of a completed dummy book, so the extent to which the publisher will want to propose changes and exert editorial influence will vary from project to project. A contract is sometimes awarded even though the publisher is not interested in publishing the book idea that has been presented. The quality of the artwork, and evidence of the maker's understanding of the picturebook format, may have been enough to convince the publisher of his or her potential.

The specific visual nature of the picturebook means editorial and design input can often overlap. In other words, the way the text and image are integrated visually has an impact on the message the book conveys. So, although the picturebook maker will work with one editor as a main point of contact, if the project is for one of the larger publishing houses he or she can expect meetings with a range of people who will have input into the development of the book. This can involve changes to the characterization, the overall structure of the sequence, use of colour – almost any aspect of the book's identity. There may be regular meetings between the company's editorial team and its sales and marketing team, particularly when it comes to the cover of the book, which will be seen to have a major bearing on its sales.

The designer

An often underappreciated contributor to the creation of a good picturebook is the designer/typographer. Although many picturebook makers play an active role in the overall design of their book, the graphic designer within a publishing house is usually key to its development. In a picturebook – where visual elements come together to create meaning – placement, harmony and graphic emphasis take on considerable importance. For an artist who is not entirely comfortable with typography and with making some of the other design decisions, a mutually trusting relationship with an in-house designer is a real bonus.

Mike Jolley is the art director at UK-based Templar Publishing, which has created a number of highly distinctive books in recent years. He has noticed a change in picturebook makers' attitudes to design in recent years.

Interestingly, the older generation of artists tends to be more relaxed about the designer's input. The younger artists have grown up with computers and are more likely to present a picturebook idea as a formed type and image creation, presenting spreads with text on, maybe with wildly inventive typography! There are certain things we have to remind them of, like the fact that the text usually has to be printed in black in order to save on the printing of translated editions. We try to have a flexible attitude, though, and usually work through things together. Just occasionally, an artist may stick stubbornly to something we don't feel will work and we have to trust our judgement and, if necessary, be prepared to walk away. But usually, if our comments are valid, they will be taken on board. On the other hand, some books can reach publication without too many changes from the original concept. Kevin Waldron's Mr Peek and the Misunderstanding at the Zoo *(Templar, 2008), for example. There were one or two editorial changes but the typographic style was pretty faithful to his original version.*

Sometimes a book evolves visually as a design idea. *The Princess' Blankets* (Templar, 2008) by Poet Laureate, Carol Ann Duffy developed in this way. The beautiful text is illustrated by a series of paintings augmented with scatterings of gold and silver foiling that have clear relevance to the content of the narrative. With *Leon and the Place Between* (Templar, 2009), with text by Angela McAllister, Grahame Baker-Smith's digital collage illustrations evolved with ongoing design input, including the use of die-cutting, special fifth-colour ink and highly integrated typography.

Reflecting on the role of the designer, Mike Jolley says he sometimes feels as though he is a tightrope walker: 'In my position I have to walk a fine line between remembering that I am employed by the publisher while also passionately championing an artist or a particular book. The publisher's view may be from the storytelling rather than primarily aesthetic perspective. Visions can inevitably sometimes become compromised. Scale or format can be an issue for example. A book that we may have envisaged in large format may get a response from the

Left: Kevin Waldron's award-winning *Mr Peek and the Misunderstanding at the Zoo* came to the publisher, Templar, as a fairly complete design concept.

marketing people along the lines of "People won't pay so much for this book. It needs to be smaller." So we need to have a rethink. But I think the designer's role is to find a way to accommodate these concerns without compromising the artist's or author's vision.'

The Bologna Children's Book Fair

Before a book is printed it is usually tested, in the form of a facsimile dummy, at a major international book fair. The Bologna Children's Book Fair is of particular importance to the industry. Publishers of children's books come together from all corners of the world to do business, to sell co-editions of their latest books, or to arrange future meetings and generally network. Here it is possible to encounter tiny independent publishers, and publishers from emerging cultures and economies alongside huge global publishing houses with massive marketing machinery. The four-day fair also gives professionals within the industry an opportunity to learn from each other and to enjoy the various exhibitions, lectures and awards ceremonies that take place alongside the main agenda of commerce.

Printing

With high-quality printing now possible all over the world, and global movement and transportation increasingly available, the key criterion in choosing a printer is often cost. Most picturebooks are now printed in the Far East where very high quality can be achieved at competitive prices because of lower labour costs. The unit cost of a print run (the cost per book) is relatively small in relation to the final sale price, which takes into account the many costs associated with the production of a book. As a rough guide, for many publishers the print unit cost needs to be around 10 per cent of the sale price to be cost-effective. The more books printed, the lower the unit cost. As the paper picturebook battles to assert itself

Left: Catherine Hyde's paintings for *The Princess' Blankets* are enhanced by various design and production decisions that included adding gold and silver foiling.

alongside screen-based alternatives, production quality is increasingly important.

Distribution

The movement of books from printer to bookshops is a major logistical issue. Many larger publishers have their own distribution operations but others employ separate companies with enormous warehouses and transport fleets.

Sales and marketing

In the larger publishing houses, sales and marketing departments play a major role in the promotion and success of a picturebook. Their people liaise with the major bookstores, the press and even schools to give publicity to, and generate interest in, the product. Many picturebook makers visit schools and bookshops on a regular basis to talk about, and sign copies of, their books. This is often organized by the publisher's marketing department.

The timing of publication can be an important factor in the success of a picturebook. Many books are themed to coincide with particular seasons and festivals, including Christmas and Halloween.

Booksellers

The final port of call on the picturebook's journey to a child's bookshelf is, of course, the place where it is sold. This may be a single independent bookshop or an outlet of a national chain. As with publishing houses, the former are now vastly outnumbered by the latter in many cultures. In the case of bookselling chains, selecting the picturebooks to be displayed and promoted in a shop may be done at national level, which provides little opportunity for the products of new, smaller publishers to gain entry. Publishers can pay major bookselling

Above: The annual Bologna Children's Book Fair is a key event in the calendar of the global children's publishing industry.

Right: Discounting and '3 for 2' offers can play a key role in the success of a picturebook.

chains to promote their books. Independent bookshops have the freedom to buy the books they wish to sell, or which they feel will appeal most to their customers. Representatives of publishing houses visit bookshops regularly, to show them the publisher's latest publications and encourage their buyers to order them. Discounting is now commonplace: '3 for 2' offers are worthwhile for publishers when they gain national exposure for books, even if profit margins are reduced. With the deregulation of selling rules in recent years, the role of supermarkets in selling books has become increasingly important. Many supermarket chains stock a small range of picturebooks – and those that are chosen are exposed to a vast buying public.

Of course, online booksellers, such as Amazon, have a major slice of the market. But browsing is particularly important when it comes to buying picturebooks, so the child-friendly bookshop still has a key role to play.

The library market

The library market is particularly important in the United States, where sales to libraries and schools can make a significant difference to the overall sales of a picturebook. Many editors have this in mind when they are commissioning.

The reviewer

Good reviews of a picturebook in major publications can be vital for the sales of the book. Publishers send new books to magazines and newspapers in the hope that they will be favourably reviewed. But how are picturebooks reviewed? They are evolving and changing so quickly as a form that it has proved difficult for reviewers to keep up with their essentially visual nature. Many reviewers come from a non-visual, literary background and are unsure how to write about them. In the United Kingdom, Nicolette Jones is children's book reviewer for the *Sunday Times* and is acutely aware of these issues:

There is a danger, particularly in short reviews, of simply retelling the story and adding a word about how nice the pictures are. Picturebooks are principally visual in their communication. For children, the story is very important, but in this context the narrative is often told visually. I receive an avalanche of books for review. I have to be drawn in to a book visually in order to feel that I want to write about it. Similarly, when people choose picturebooks to buy, apart from occasionally looking for a book that addresses a particular subject, they will usually select on the basis of what is visually engaging.

I suppose reviewing is essentially an individual, idiosyncratic thing, but it is also partly objective. I think you can judge quality as with any form of literature. I like to think that I can sometimes point out works of real quality. Left entirely to their own devices, young children will pick up something that makes a noise or has an element that they recognize from the TV. But we wouldn't leave children to choose sweets or burgers all the time, so it is equally important to help them find books that are nourishing and will have lasting quality. We all spend a great deal of time looking at fast images now. Slow images are important. Children are naturally visual. They have a powerful capacity to look and to absorb images. It's something that we can lose as we get older. Visual thinking is important, not just if you are an artist, but in anything. You have to be visually aware in order to write. Picturebooks are important!

Case study: The publisher's perspective

Random House and Nadia Shireen

Helen MacKenzie Smith is editorial director for picturebooks at Random House Children's Books in London. She has been responsible for publishing a number of exciting new talents in recent years including Alexis Deacon, Katie Cleminson and Nadia Shireen. MacKenzie Smith explains how she goes about finding new talent:

It's about fifty-fifty – attending graduation shows and being sent samples. I do try to look at all of it. For example, Katie Cleminson sent in samples including her 'Box of Tricks' idea. I opened it and immediately loved it. I telephoned her straight away. She was a bit shocked, I think. I suppose it's an instinctive thing. The more difficult part is knowing how to say 'no' to people with the sheer volume of stuff sent in. I'm always interested if people demonstrate a knowledge of what we publish. I remember when Louise Yates first made contact, she was a fan of Alexis Deacon's work. It's a good idea to know who's publishing the books that you really love. Sending your

Right: Early storyboard for *The Good Little Wolf*.

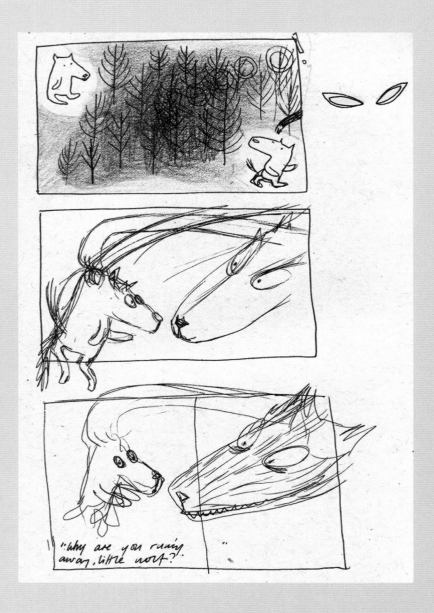

"why are you running away, little wolf?"

website address in is OK. It doesn't mean it gets seen any quicker though.

When it comes to picturebooks I would say that it's quite rare to get good artwork and good writing together. When it happens, as in the ones I've mentioned, you just get this intangible sense of 'She's got it!'. And as an editor, you've got to really love the book to get it through the system to publication. You've got to be able to champion it.

The people to be persuaded can be numerous. As described above, they can include those in editorial, design, sales, marketing and publicity right through to the sales reps who take the books out to shops, and finally the bookshops who have to persuade people to buy them. For British publishers, selling books to the American market has been very important. With the global recession of recent years, this has become more challenging. As MacKenzie Smith explains:

In times of recession the word 'classic' has a particular resonance. It's a lot harder to sell books that are scary or challenging. Everyone is more cautious about anything new. We have good working relationships with particular publishers in the US, Knopf for example, who publish Mini Grey. I have to ask people to trust me on new books. I focus on about ten books a year.

On what she'd like to see for picturebooks in the future, MacKenzie Smith says:

Well I'd love to see more picturebooks for older children getting through. Picturebooks don't have to be just for the three- to seven year-olds. I'd like to see hardbacks surviving more, too. In the UK they are very difficult to sell. I'd like to see more books breaking out of the 32-page format. We do need to take a few more risks. There is a tendency for one extraordinary book to emerge and then everyone follows the format until it's dead. With all of these things you need the seller who will push them. I think we need to value picturebooks as part of our culture much more. Initiatives such as Quentin Blake's new 'House of Illustration' will certainly help.

This page and opposite: Nadia Shireen's *The Good Little Wolf* caused something of a feeding frenzy among publishers on her graduation in 2010. Eventually, the author settled with Random House, a decision based on personalities; both parties felt comfortable with each other.

Passionate about picturebooks, MacKenzie Smith is a committee member for the Big Picture, an organization devoted to raising awareness of the genre. As she says, many adults have little sense of what the word really means: 'Someone asked me the other day what on earth there is to do as a picturebook editor – "Surely there aren't enough words?" It put me in mind of the famous quotation – "I would have written you a shorter letter but I didn't have the time."'[2]

MacKenzie Smith first encountered the work of Nadia Shireen at the latter's graduation exhibition in London in early 2010. Shireen's book, *The Good Little Wolf*, had been produced as her final project for her masters degree in children's book illustration at Anglia Ruskin University.

At her graduation show Shireen was lucky enough to be pursued by a number of publishers, but ultimately chose to accept an offer from MacKenzie Smith at Random House. As she explains, the reasons for her choice were not primarily financial: 'I think it was mostly gut instinct. I knew that whoever I would be working with, we would need to be comfortable about working closely together, to feel like we are on the same wavelength.'

Shireen took time to speak to all of the interested parties and also to take advice on the details of the various contracts offered: 'But there was a calmness about our conversations that was very reassuring. Also, I grew up with Roald Dahl and Quentin Blake. They had a major influence on my childhood so I think the fact that this was the same publisher also had an effect.'

---

[2] Variously attributed to Blaise Pascal or Mark Twain.

Case study: Growing a publishing business

Thierry Magnier

Editions TM in Paris is one of the best-known publishers for children in France. The books are published in numerous languages and Thierry Magnier, who set up the company, is in great demand as a speaker and international jury member. His publishing empire now includes Actes Sud and the highly influential Editions du Rouergue.

Prior to working in children's publishing, Magnier studied horticulture and worked as a florist and a gardener. He also studied education, science and psychology, and went on to work as a schoolteacher. He says: 'I think I was a subversive teacher. I decided to leave teaching as I was too free-spirited. I met friends who had opened a bookshop. I opened two bookshops in Normandy and ran these for five years.'

In the bookshops Magnier specialized in children's literature, working with teachers and children to promote reading and the imagination. He then returned to Paris to take on the role of communications director for the Association of Bookshops. After a while, he set up a newspaper called *Page* and later another for children, *Petit Page*, promoting children's literature. He left to work at Gallimard with the legendary Pierre Marchand, who had initiated the children's publishing section in 1972. Once again, itchy feet got the better of him and he left to set up Editions TM, which has quickly established itself as a highly

Right and opposite: *Tout un monde* and *rendez-vous n'importe òu* have been big-selling titles from Editions TM.

KATY COUPRIE
ANTONIN LOUCHARD

Tout un monde

EDITIONS THIERRY MAGNIER

successful publishing house. Magnier finds time to teach on various masters courses and to write novels. He is also working with psychiatrists on a project researching the baby's relationship with books.

Speaking about his personal philosophy in relation to publishing for children, Magnier says:

It's instinct and intuition really. I have this passion for cooking and gardening, and there are many parallels. A picturebook has many ingredients, harmony of colour and flavour. And it is about sharing and about presentation, about finding the right ingredients, flavours and textures. My philosophy also involves always looking for something new. With a new picturebook maker it is important that he or she feels total ownership of the book, but also appreciates that it is a team project. There is no standard recipe for a good book, but a good book for children is also a good book for adults. The more ingredients and layers there are, the more levels or ages it will reach.

It is generally perceived that picturebooks in France have, in recent years, been especially innovative visually. Magnier feels it has been possible to take risks, but that this is becoming more difficult. He does not publish 'series books'.

I have too great an appetite for something new. Of course, I would like to make lots of money but it is never possible to predict the big successes. When I prepare a book I try to make it a beautiful book. When a book has big success, it allows a little more risk with another book. Each new book I am in love with as it is in preparation. You have to believe in a book to publish it.

On the subject of electronic or eBooks, he feels that technology cannot be resisted but that it will simply help define the qualities that make paper picturebooks special: 'It becomes even more important to make even more beautiful books. The book is a physical object, a material, sensual thing to feel and touch.'

Case study: Small, independent publishers

Media Vaca, Topipittori and De Eenhoorn

Although, as in many industries, children's publishing has become increasingly dominated by large conglomerates, small independent publishers continue to flourish. They are often created by one or two individuals with a passion for quality visual literature and its important role in the intellectual and cultural development of the child. Frequently, it is these small publishing houses that introduce new and innovative visual approaches and ideas to the picturebook world. Without the need to convince layers of marketing and sales people of a book's commercial potential, there is much more likelihood that books that have not been 'designed by committee' will emerge. It is no accident that the majority of books awarded the Bologna Ragazzi Award for Fiction have, in recent years, emerged from small-scale set-ups.

Media Vaca ('half a cow') is based in Valencia, Spain, and was formed in 1998 by Vicente Ferrer Azcoiti and Begoña Lòb Abascal. Since then, Vicente Ferrer and Abascal have created highly distinctive books, their small flow of carefully considered and beautifully produced publications increasing only slightly over the years. Apart from printing, everything is done in-house.

In many ways, Media Vaca is redefining the concept of the picturebook. All the books are hardback with dust jackets. They are shaped like traditional hardback novels for adults but

Below left, top: Vicente Ferrer Azcoiti and Begoña Lobo Abascal, founders of Media Vaca, at their offices in Valencia, Spain (photo: Daniel Garcia-Sala).

Below left, bottom: The Media Vaca logo: half a cow.

Below right and opposite: *No Hay Tiempo Para Jugar*/No Time to Play (text Sandra Arenal, illustrations Mariana Chiesa; Media Vaca, 2004). Produced in typical Media Vaca hardback format, the book gives voice to the child labourers of Mexico in words and pictures.

the imagery always plays as important a role as the text. The number of pages is usually far greater than in the standard picturebook. Vicente Ferrer says:

I don't understand this thing called a 'picturebook'. What is it? It's a commercial thing. Most of the texts are stupid! In Spain we still have many teachers who write picturebooks with subjects such as 'the family' and so on. Children can be turned off reading by this experience. They are not poets, they are teachers!

Vicente Ferrer originally worked as an illustrator. This may partly explain his passion for the visual and production quality of books, but he is equally passionate about the importance of content – visual and verbal text:

If we think of the first artists in their caves – they would paint a picture of a buffalo. But it is the idea of the buffalo that matters. The idea is that you want food – a buffalo in the stomach. Saul Steinberg wrote his ideas in pictures. Goya knew how to make narrative artworks. His paintings are movies. You need to spend time to read them. He was the greatest of illustrators. If the illustrations do not say anything, it is preferable to have a book with blank pages, in order to imagine better things. Children should have the very best books – the best stories, the best drawings, the best paper. The size of the book is very important to me. It is a matter of respect for the reader. And you cannot ask good artists to work in a small space.

Vicente Ferrer and Abascal explain that in Spain, the concept of the picturebook is a relatively recent one:

You would buy the next book in a well-known series. These would be small, paperback books with only the writer's name on the cover. The status of the artist had been much higher in the 1930s, before the civil war. After Franco's death in 1975, some books began to be imported and translated.

We started by making only three books a year. We still have a very small output. We currently have 12 books in production. I can't produce catalogues because I never know when anything will be ready!

Most of the books are the brainchild of the publisher. They are often obscure texts that Vicente Ferrer discovers lurking in previously drab packaging, and he does justice to them by making them into books more worthy of their content:

Sometimes the text is very small. I choose an artist and invite them to help me make this into a more important book. I am motivated by curiosity. Humour is important to me, too. Our

NOS BRINCAN LOS GRANDES

En mi casa somos cuatro hermanos, una hermana, mi papá y mi mamá. Yo tengo 12 años, estudio en las mañanas y vengo en las tardes a empacar la mercancía. Voy a completar el año. Saco entre 12 y 15.000 pesos diarios. En mi casa trabajan mi papá en la obra y mi mamá en una casa; yo soy el otro que trabaja. A mí se me ocurrió un día que oí a unos chavos hablar de esto. Tengo un hermano mayor que estudia comercio. Él no trabaja porque está dedicado a sus estudios; ya se va a recibir. Ahorita estamos juntando para su graduación. Ya mero termina, luego se pondrá a trabajar. Los otros hermanitos van a la escuela, y sólo mi hermana la más chica va al kinder.

Me gusta este trabajo porque la gente nos trata bien. Bueno, la mayoría: sólo de vez en cuando le tocan a uno señoras enojonas, pero son pocas. Los supervisores son buena onda, pero muy exigentes. Debemos ser puntuales; tenemos que venir bien limpios, con corbata y el uniforme completo; traer delantal, que nosotros mismos compramos o los hacemos. Yo me hice éste, por eso está un poco chueco, pero ya puesto no se nota.

Aquí nadie se pelea, porque si lo hacemos ya no nos dejan venir. Y otra cosa es que debe uno ser buen alumno, si no ya no nos dejan trabajar. Hasta credencial nos dieron, y se la quitan a uno cuando hacemos algo malo, sobre todo a los que se pelean; por eso nadie lo hace. Nos aguantamos, aunque a veces nos brinquen los más grandes –porque hacemos fila para pasar–; mejor nos aguantamos que decirles algo, porque si no nos amuelan.

Soriana en Navidad nos hace una posada con payasos y nos regala un juguete. Eso es lo que la empresa nos da. ¡Es bien padre!

RAÚL, 12 años, trabaja en Almacenes Soriana de empacador.

53

books are for children but are often about children too, in the same way as the books of Charles Dickens.

Like Media Vaca, Topipittori in Milan is a publishing house that has evolved from a design background with a strong interest in the visual. Paulo Canton and Giovanna Zoboli created the company in 2004. Canton had wide experience of working with illustrators when he designed promotional brochures and small books as editions of corporate gifts. The company now publishes eight to ten picturebooks for children and young adults each year, and its books have won numerous international awards. Its stated aim is '… to produce picturebooks which can contribute to the intellectual and emotional growth of children'.

Canton's and Zoboli's spacious apartment and offices are filled with light and with books. Canton explains that he has always been interested in text and image, and has a substantial collection of antiquarian books, especially herbals. This is a publisher with an unusual sensitivity to the art of the picturebook.

Speaking about the various ways books come into being, Canton says:

Sometimes people come to us with a project. Sometimes we have an idea that we want to pursue. Often publishers have a strong idea of how they want things to be, but I prefer to find a way into an individual artist's world. A book that we are working on at the moment comes from an experience we had when we were visiting the village where Giovanna grew up. It was a saint's day and in the village a man was selling balloons in the shapes of animals. It was visually magical and we wanted to make this into a picturebook. We invited Beatrice Alemagna to develop it. Beatrice felt it important that Giovanna should write the story.

Inevitably, with such a focus on quality, some have described Topipittori books as difficult. Canton's view on this is particularly interesting:

Below: *Libro de las Preguntas*/Book of Questions (text Pablo Neruda, illustrations Isidro Ferrer; Media Vaca, 2006). Ferrer's three-dimensional assemblages perfectly complement Neruda's philosophical questions in another Media Vaca book that stretches the traditional perception of 'picturebook'.

LII

Cuánto medía el pulpo negro
que oscureció la paz del día?

Eran de hierro sus ramales
y de fuego muerto sus ojos?

Y la ballena tricolor
por qué me atajó en el camino?

Well, I think we always have doubts about what we do. Doubts are important. And I'm always disappointed with a book – I always feel it could have been better. But I'm not sure about the idea of 'difficulty'. Nothing is too difficult for children. I think it was Walter Benjamin who said that he had to learn to read by reading the Bible. Certainly, I am always wrong if I try to predict what will be commercially successful. It is strange that parents seem to consider the book to be the last place where children have the right of choice. Most people would not allow a child to choose to eat burgers and sweets all day yet it seems OK to allow a poor visual diet. I saw a programme on TV the other day where experts were trying to understand why a three-year-old was still speaking in baby talk. It turned out that the child's mother was still speaking to her in baby talk. This is what often happens in books – the complexity of the world is reduced to pictorial baby talk. We are compelled to suggest age groups for our books on our catalogue but it's senseless really. I would prefer to say that our books are for 'persons'.

This approach has clearly not been detrimental to strong business growth for Topipittori. The company doubled its turnover in 2008 and, despite the recession, business was still up by 30 per cent in 2009. A strong presence at international book fairs such as Bologna (where the company teamed up with the like-minded Portuguese publisher Planeta Tangerina in 2010) has been important for co-edition sales. In Italy, there are around 2,000 bookshops and four major bookselling chains, plus some mixed stationery/general shops and a reasonably strong network of smaller independent bookshops. Topipittori's books have a presence in about 250 of the bookshops.

Marita Vermeulen's route into the world of children's book publishing was slightly different. De Eenhoorn of Belgium is another company with a strong focus on high-quality artwork. Vermeulen's background is as a writer and critic of many years experience. She has long been a champion of Flemish picturebook makers and wrote the text for *Colouring Outside the Lines*, which accompanied a touring exhibition of the work

Below: *L'angelo delle scarpe*/The Shoe Angel (text Giovanna Zoboli, illustrations Joanna Concejo; Topipittori, 2009). An aesthetic treat, this book brings together highly poetic text and illustration. Topipittori market these books as 'crickets in the head'– 'books written and illustrated to open windows on hidden meanings…'

of Flemish picturebook artists. Her passion for picturebook art led her to take a course in illustration, in order to better understand the processes involved in creative practice. She now combines her publishing activities with part-time teaching of illustration at KASK, the Royal Academy of Fine Arts in Ghent. Here she works alongside the artist Carll Kneut, whose distinctive and distinguished work she regularly publishes. Kneut's most recent project, *Het Geheim van de Keel van de Nachtegaal* – a retelling of Hans Christian Andersen's *The Nightingale* with a text by Peter Verhelst (2009) – has been very successful. The book is a beautifully produced hardback of (pages) with gold printing on the paper edges and no expense spared. Vermeulen explains:

Carll has gone further with his work on this book. We are very proud of it. As it evolved, the book became more and more expensive to produce. People were telling me that I would bankrupt the company! But it has been a great success and it's reassuring to know that so-called difficult and expressive books can do well. People go for the beauty of this book. They fall in love with this book. I want to make books that people fall in love with! This is a book that you look at over and over again. If you look at the best paintings that still have meaning today, they are narrative. As a publisher, I want to make room to let the unexpected happen. If I lose the ability to be enchanted by a book, I will go and work in a warehouse. When illustrators come to see me, I want them to leave with the feeling that the

Left: Beatrice Alemagna's *Che Cos'è un Bambino?/What is a Child?* (Topipittori, 2008) has been a major success for the publisher.

possibilities have increased. If you don't allow an illustrator this increased space, you suffocate them. You may get a couple of OK books, but you lose the possibility of excellence. When meeting new artists it is important to know whether I can work with someone. It's not just about talent. It's about stamina, empathy, a flair for communication – not just as an illustrator but as a human being. Doubt is important too; doubt goes with curiosity. I do try to instil confidence in students, though, in the sense of having belief that they can make a good book.

The Flemish Literature Fund plays an important role in occasionally funding the production of books and sometimes subsidizing picturebook artists. As with similar arrangements in countries such as Norway, this can lead to a less commercially

driven approach to art for children. Vermeulen has clear views on books for this market:

In some countries there can be a tendency to overprotect children and only give them a sort of fragrant Kate Greenaway world; like a sort of sleeping pill if you like. As adults, we do often want to protect too much. When we have worked directly with children and our books, as we did with Isabelle Vandenabeele's Rood Rood Roodkapje *(De Eenhoorn, 2003) for instance, the children loved the book but parents said 'No – it will frighten you!' In a way, it's a little like countries where we see oppression of women.*

Left: Isabelle Vandenabeele's graphically sinister version of Red Riding Hood for De Eenhoorn (text Edward van de Vendel) caused some concern among parents, but was well received by children.

Below: This lavish production of Peter Verhelst's retelling of Andersen's *The Nightingale*, with illustrations by Carll Kneut, proved to be a big success for De Eenhoorn despite being more expensive than originally planned.

The eBook developer

Jon Skuse originally worked in the computer games industry, then took an MA in children's book illustration to develop his illustration skills. He now works as a freelance developer with a range of picturebook publishers, helping them to move into the world of eBooks. With his background, he is uniquely equipped to observe the relationship between the traditional and digital picturebook. As he explains:

There are two aspects to this – the business side and the creative side. The eBook is cheap to make once the technology is in place and it is cheap to buy. And you are not limited to a certain number of pages in the way a print-based book is. It doesn't have to be linear in its construction either. The creator can make different 'branches' or routes; for example, the reader can tap on a door to take one route or tap on another to follow a different narrative.

This, of course, begs the question about where the picturebook ends and the game begins. Skuse believes that there is a clear distinction:

The eBook isn't about winning or losing. It's about an 'exploration', an experience, rather like a pop-up book. What many publishers are doing wrong at the moment is just copying printed picturebooks on to this format, which does both media a disservice. It's just like looking at a PDF. Children will simply flick through. A printed picturebook is a particular kind of physical experience that can be savoured and revisited. The eBook needs to exploit its own particular characteristics and strengths to evolve as similarly special but distinct experience.

Below: Picturebooks are now being developed specifically for the screen, as seen here in the form of content from the publisher WingedChariot. They can be downloaded quickly and comparatively cheaply. It remains to be seen whether this will provide a viable stream of income for the authors.

Scruffy Kitty makes me laugh.

The future

It is clear that the picturebook will continue to evolve. The impact of the emergence of the eBook and iPad will, as with most technological developments, partly redefine and also coexist with their ancestor. Reading on screen will undoubtedly become an increasingly popular (and, arguably, more environmentally friendly) alternative to reading on paper, particularly in the context of information and news. It may be the case, however, that the picturebook will be the most dogged survivor on paper; its intimate and aesthetic physical relationship with parent and child is less suited to the screen. Indeed, it may well continue to distinguish itself from the screen by becoming increasingly assertive in its physical three-dimensional form. Picturebooks will become ever more lavishly and beautifully produced.

For the all-round health of the picturebook publishing industry, it is vital that small publishers continue to flourish alongside the larger houses, taking risks and nourishing the industry as a whole. If new generations of innovative picturebook makers are to emerge, passionate publishers such as those described above will be essential. In an interview with John Burningham, Deborah Orr asked him about today's approach to publishing picturebooks. Burningham responded:

… they have so many restrictions now. They have very good editors out there, very good production people… but it's committee-led. You have to get a committee to pass everything… the accountants, the salesmen, the marketing people. I'm in the lucky position where I can do what I want and just get on with it, but I don't know what I'd do if I had to start now.

Orr reflects:

In many ways, the vision of childhood that Burningham and other young artists portrayed in their ground-breaking picturebooks has gone the same way as the publishing houses who championed them with such passion. The need for work like Burningham's is as urgent now, if not more, than it was back in 1962.[3]

Indeed it is. And that work is out there, with new generations of innovative picturebook makers emerging from all corners of the world, nourishing and reinvigorating the children's publishing industry.

Perhaps the last word (or, rather, the last word and picture) should go to that modern master of the idiom, Lane Smith. In his new picturebook, *It's a Book* (Roaring Brook Press, 2010), Smith's ape tries to explain to Jackass that the thing he is holding is called a book. Among the stream of questions asked by Jackass are: 'How do you scroll down?', 'Does it need a password?', 'Can you tweet?' and 'Can you make the characters fight?'. When Jackass eventually gets the hang of this strange object, ape is forced to enquire 'Are you going to give my book back?'. 'No', replies Jackass.

[3] *Independent*, 18 April 2009.

IT'S A BOOK, JACKASS.

Above: Lane Smith explores the clash
of cultures between paper and screen in
It's a Book.

Related reading and browsing

The following is a list of books, periodicals and websites relating to the making and the study of picturebooks. It is by no means comprehensive, but it is a starting point.

Books

Alderson, B.
Sing a Song for Sixpence: The English Picture Book Tradition and Randolph Caldecott
Cambridge University Press, 1986

Alderson, B. and de Marez Oyens, F.
Be Merry and Wise: Origins of Children's Publishing in England, 1650–1850
The Pierpoint Morgan Library, The Bibliographical Society of America, The British Library London, Oak Knoll Press, Newcastle, 2006

Amos, B. and Suben, E.
Writing and Illustrating Children's Books for Publication: Two Perspectives
Writer's Digest Books, 2005

Arizpe, E. and Styles, M.
Children Reading Pictures: Interpreting Visual Texts
RoutledgeFalmer, 2003

Backemeyer, S. (ed.)
Picture This: the Artist as Illustrator
A & C Black, 2005

Baddeley, P. and Eddershaw, C.
Not so Simple Picture Books: Developing Responses to Literature with 4–12-Year-olds
Trentham Books, 1994

Baines, P.
Puffin by Design: 70 Years of Imagination 1940–2010
Allen Lane, 2010

Barr, J.
Illustrated Children's Books
The British Library, 1980

Blake, Q.
Magic Pencil: Children's Book Illustration Today
The British Library, 2002

Blake, Q.
Words and Pictures
Jonathan Cape, 2000

Bland, D.
A History of Book Illustration: The Illuminated Manuscript and the Printed Book
Faber & Faber, 1958

Bland, D.
The Illustration of Books
Faber & Faber 1951

Chester, T. R.
Children's Book Research: A Practical Guide to Techniques and Sources
Thimble Press/Westminster College 1989

Colomer, T., Kümmerling, B. and Silva-Diaz, C. (eds)
New Directions in Picture Book Research
Routledge, 2010

Cummins, J. (ed.)
Children's Book Illustration and Design Vol 2
PBC International Inc, 1998

Dalphin, M., Mahony Miller, B. and Viguers, R. H.
Illustrators of Children's Books 1946–1956
Horn Book Co, 1958

Doonan, J.
Looking at Pictures in Picture Books
Thimble Press, 1993

Evans, D.
Show and Tell: Exploring the Fine Art of Children's Book Illustration
Chronicle Books, 2008

Evans, J.
What's in the Picture? Responding to Illustrations in Picture Books
Sage Publications Ltd, 1998

Fisher, M.
Who's Who in Children's Books: a Treasury of the Familiar Characters of Childhood
Weidenfeld and Nicolson, 1975

Gauch, G. L., Briggs, D. and Palmer, C.
Artist to Artist: 23 Major Illustrators Talk About Their Art
Philomel Books, 2007

Gibson, M.
'Picturebooks, comics and graphic novels' in Rudd, D. (ed.) *The Routledge Companion to Children's Literature,* pp. 100–111
Routledge, 2010

Graham, J.
Pictures on the Page
National Association for the Teaching of English, 1990

Harding, J. and Pinsent, P. (eds)
What do You See? International Perspectives on Children's Book Illustration
Cambridge Scholars Publishing, 2008

Heller, S. and Arisman, M.
The Education of an Illustrator
Allworth Press, 2000

Herdog, W. (ed.)
Graphis 155. Special Issue: Children's Books
1972

Herdog, W. (ed.)
Graphis 177. Special Issue: Children's Books
1976

Horne, A. (ed.)
The Dictionary of Twentieth Century British Book Illustrators
Antique Collectors' Club, 1994

Hunt, P., Sainsbury, L. and McCorquodale, D.
Illustrated Children's Books
Black Dog Publishing, 2009

Hürlimann, B.
Three Centuries of Children's Books in Europe
World Publishing Company, 1968

Hürlimann, B. (Brian Alderson, trans. and ed.)
Picture Book World
Oxford University Press, 1968

Kiefer, B. Z.
The Potential of Picture Books
Merrill/Prentice Hall, 1995

Kingman, L.
Newberry and Caldecott Medal Books 1976–1985
Horn Books, 1985

Kingman, L.
Newberry and Caldecott Medal Books 1966–1975
Horn Books, 1975

Kingman, L., Foster, J., Lontoft, R. G. (eds)
Illustrators of Children's Books: 1957–1966
Horn Books, 1968

Kingman, L.
The Illustrator's Notebook
Horn Books, 1978

Klemin, D.
The Illustrated Book: Its Art and Craft
Clarkson N. Potter inc, 1970

Klemin, D.
The Art of Art for Children's Books
Clarkson N. Potter, 1966

Kress, G. and Van Leeuwen, T.
Reading Images: The Grammar of Visual Design
Routledge, 1996

Kushner, T.
The Art of Maurice Sendak: 1980 to the Present
Harry N. Abrams, 2003

Lacy, L. E.
Art & Design in Children's Picture Books: an analysis of Caldecott Award-winning illustrations
ALA Editions, 1986

Lanes, S. G.
The Art of Maurice Sendak
Abradale Press/Harry N. Abrams Inc, 1980

Lanes, S. G.
Through the Looking Glass: Further Adventures and Misadventures in the Realm of Children's Literature
David R. Godine, 2004

Lewis, D.
Reading contemporary Picturebooks: Picturing Text
RoutledgeFalmer, 2001

Lewis, J.
The Twentieth Century Book
The Herbert Press, 1984 (revised edition)

Marantz, S. and Marantz, K. A.
The Art of Children's Picture Books: a Selective Reference Guide
Taylor and Francis, 1988

Marantz, K. A. and Marantz, S.
Creating Picture Books: Interviews with Editors, Art Directors, Reviewers, Professors, Librarians and Showcasers
McFarland & Co Inc, 1998

Marantz, K. A. and Marantz, S.
Multicultural Picture Books: Art for Illuminating Our World
Scarecrow Press, 2004 (2nd edition)

Marantz, K. A. and Marantz, S.
Artists of the Page: Interviews with Children's Book Illustrators
McFarland & Co Inc, 1992

Marcus, L. S.
Ways of Telling: Conversations on the Art of the Picture Book
Dutton, 2002

McCannon, D., Thornton, S. and Williams, Y.
The Bloomsbury Guide to Creating Illustrated Children's Books
Perseus Books, 2008

McCannon, D., Thornton, S. and Williams, Y.
The Encyclopedia of Writing and Illustrating Children's Books
A & C Black, 2008

Meek, M.
How Texts Teach What Readers Learn
Thimble Press, 1988

Metaphors of Childhood (catalogue of exhibition, Bologna 2009)
Editrice Compositiri, 2009

Miller, B. M. and Field, E. W. (eds)
Newberry Medal Books 1922–1955
Horn Books, 1955

Muir, P.
English Children's Books, 1600–1900
Batsford, 1954

Nikolajeva, M. and Scott, C.
How Picture Books Work
Routledge, 2006

Noble, G., Rabey, K. and Styles, M.
Picture This! Picture Book Art at the Millennium
Fitzwilliam Museum, Cambridge, 2000

Noble, I. and Bestley, R.
Visual Research: an Introduction to Research Methodologies in Graphic Design
AVA, 2005

Nodelman, P.
Words About Pictures: the Narrative Art of Children's Picture Books
University of Georgia Press, 1990

Powers, A.
Children's Book Covers
Mitchell Beazley, 2003

Salisbury, M.
Illustrating Children's Books: Creating Pictures for Publication
A & C Black, 2004

Salisbury, M.
Play Pen: New Children's Book Illustration
Laurence King Publishing, 2007

Schwarcz, J. H.
Ways of the Illustrator: Visual Communication in Children's Literature
American Library Association, 1982

Schwarcz, J. H. and Schwarcz, C.
The Picture Book Comes of Age
American Library Association, 1991

Sendak, M.
Caldecott & Co: Notes on Books and Pictures
Farrar, Strauss & Giroux, 1988

Shulevitz, U.
Writing With Pictures: How to Write and Illustrate Children's Books
Watson-Guptill, 1985

Silvey, A. (ed.)
Children's Books and their Creators
Houghton Mifflin, 1995

Simon, F. (ed.)
The Children's Writers and Artists Year Book
A & C Black (annual)

Sipe, R. and Pantaleo, S. (eds)
Postmodern Picturebooks: Play, Parody, and Self-Referentiality
Routledge, 2008

Spaulding, A. E.
The Page as a Stage Set: Story Board Picture Books
Scarecrow Press, 1995

Spitz, E. H.
Inside Picture Books
Yale University Press, 1997

Steinev, E.
Stories for Little Comrades: Revolutionary Artists and the Making of Early Soviet Children's Books
University of Washington Press, 1999

Styles, M. and Bearne, E. (eds)
Art, Narrative and Childhood
Trentham Books, 2003

Sutherland, Z. and Arbuthnot, M. H.
Children and Books
HarperCollins, 1991

Trumpener, K.
Picture-book worlds and ways of seeing in
Grenby, M. and Immel, A. (eds) *The Cambridge Companion to Children's Literature*
Cambridge: CUP pp. 55–75 (2009)

Van der Linden, S.
Livre L'Album
L'Atelier du Poisson Soluble, 2006

Vermeulen, M.
Colouring Outside the Lines: Flemish Illustrators Making Their Mark
Flemish Literature Fund, 2003

Watson, V. and Styles, M.
Talking Pictures: Pictorial Texts and Young Readers
Hodder Arnold H & S, 1996

Whalley, J. I and Chester, T. R.
A History of Children's Book Illustration
John Murray/Victoria and Albert Museum, 1988

Wintle, J. and Fisher, E.
The Pied Pipers: Interviews with the Influential Creators of Children's Literature
Paddington Press, 1974

Withrow, S. and Withrow, L. B.
Illustrating Children's Picture Books
RotoVision 2009

Young, Timothy G.
Drawn to Enchant: Original Children's Book Art in the Beinbecke Shirley Collection
Yale University Press, 2007

Periodicals

Bookbird
Children's Literature in Education
IRSCL online journal
The Lion and the Unicorn
New Review of Children's Literature and Librarianship
INIS
Books for Keeps online
Carousel
The Story of Picture Books (S. Korea)
The Bookseller

Websites

www.alma.se/en
www.anglia.ac.uk/ruskin/en/home/microsites/ccbs.html
www.associazioneillustratori.it
www.autrement.com
www.beatricealemagna.com
www.bolognafiere.it
www.bookbrunch.co.uk
www.booktrustchildrensbooks.org.uk/Picture-Books
www.carlemuseum.org
www.chihiro.jp
www.childrensillustrators.com
www.corraini.com
www.dibuixamunconte.blogspot.com
www.elblogdeilustrarte.blogspot.com
www.elblogdepencil.wordpress.com
www.ibby.org
www.ilustrarte.es
www.ilustrarte.net
www.itabashiartmuseum.jp
www.lerouergue.com
www.metm.co.jp
www.orechioacerbo.com
www.oqo.es
www.picturingbooks.com
www.sarmedemostra.it
www.scbwi.org
www.sevenstories.org.uk
www.teatrio.it
www.thelightbox.org.uk
www.theweeweb.co.uk
www.topipittori.it
www.ucalgary.ca/~dkbrown
www.unaflordepapel.blogspot.com
www.zazienews.blogspot.com
www.zoolibri.com

Glossary

Advance ('against royalties') Initial payment to the artist/author for a picturebook. This may be broken down into two or three installments. If a book ultimately sells enough copies to exceed this initial royalty payment, then actual royalty payments to the author commence.

Adaptations When an original text appears in many different forms. For example, Briggs' wordless picturebook, *The Snowman*, has been adapted into an animated film. Images from both texts have been marketed for a myriad of commercial purposes.

Board book Picturebook for very young children, printed on stiff boards and with fewer pages than the standard 32-page picturebook.

Co-editions Editions of a book that are published in other countries and languages than that of origin.

Contract Agreement of terms and conditions drawn up between, and signed by, picturebook creator(s) and publisher.

Copyright Exclusive legal right to print or publish.

Counterpoint Often used in a musical context to describe the art of combining melodies in such a way that they 'speak' to each other and to the audience. In the context of the picturebook, the term usually refers to the dynamic between words and pictures.

'Crossover books' Books that straddle or do not fall easily into an identified age or genre category.

Décalage A French word meaning 'gap' or 'shift'. Sometimes used to describe the way that the meanings of words and pictures on a double-page spread in a picturebook can deliberately contradict or challenge each other.

Dummy An early version or 'model' of a picturebook that is made initially by the artist as a 'maquette' of the book to aid the development of its design, pace and rhythm. Later, a more finished dummy may be made up by the publisher prior to final printing, in order to present at book fairs to potential co-publishers.

Endpapers The first and last pages of a book, immediately inside the covers.

Font A set of type of one particular design or 'face'.

Gutter The margin or fold at the centre of a double-page spread.

Intertextuality When one text makes reference to another text, which might be in the form of the written word, illustration, media text or wider cultural forms. In other words, meaning does not reside purely within any given text but from its relationships with other texts and/or cultural forms.

ISBN International Standard Book Number. A unique number that identifies each book and is also included in the barcode.

Laminating Applying a transparent or coloured plastic film to the printing, often in gloss, in order to enhance or protect the surface.

Literary agent An agent who represents authors and sometimes picturebook 'makers', promoting them to publishers in return for a percentage of the income from contracts gained.

Metafiction Any work which highlights its own fictive nature. Metafictive picturebooks tend to be funny and ironic. *The Stinky Cheese Man* is a prime example, where the author and illustrator show the constructed nature of the text by playfully sending up of all the usual expectations from the title page to the back cover.

Multimodal In the context of the picturebook, this is a term used to describe the plurality of modes of communication: e.g. words and pictures.

Novelty books Books that are characterized by novelty elements such as pop-up, fold-out or other moving parts.

Paratext According to Genette (1997), this consists of all the information extraneous to the central text itself. The term is often divided into **peritext** – all the information in a text that is not part of the central 'story' such as author's name, publishing details, blurb, dust cover, preface, endpapers…; and the **epitext** consisting of elements outside the actual volume such as advertising, reviews and interview.

Postmodernism This is a contested term which resists categorization. In the field of picturebooks, it tends to refer to narratives which often have many of the following features: playfulness, rule-breaking, indeterminacy, ambiguity, fragmentation, incompleteness, etc. It is worth noting that many children take such challenges in their stride.

Recto Right-hand page of an open book.

Reprint Printing of the book that is subsequent to the first printing.

Rough An unfinished, simplified version of a design, drawing or layout.

Royalties Amount received by artist and/or author as a percentage of the income from sales of a book.

Spread Printed matter across two facing pages.

Storyboard A sequence of miniature frames on a single sheet of paper on which the picturebook maker initially plans out the structure and sequence of the picturebook.

Title page Normally the recto page after the opening endpapers of a picturebook, carrying the title and decorative motifs.

Verso Left-hand page of an open book.

Index

Acknowledgements

Thanks are due first of all to Pam Smy for her tireless assistance with picture permissions. Thanks too to Laurence King Publishing, especially to Melanie Walker for her careful and considerate editing, to Donald Dinwiddie for his generous support and organization and to Studio Ten and a Half for their sensitive design. Gratitude is also extended to the many MA Children's Book Illustration students at Cambridge School of Art who have allowed their work to be studied and reproduced, and to all those busy publishers and editors who gave up their time to speak to us. Finally, thanks to Beatrice Alemagna for her beautiful artwork for the cover.

Picture credits

Every effort has been made to contact the copyright holders, but should there be any errors or omissions the publishers would be pleased to insert the appropriate acknowledgement in any subsequent edition of the book. Items in bold refer to page number and position.

10 © The Bridgeman Art Library. **11** © Vincenzo Pirozzi, Rome – fotopirozzi@inwind.it. **12 (right)** © Fitzwilliam Museum, University of Cambridge/ The Bridgeman Art Library. **18** *Clever Bill* © William Nicholson, 1926. **19** *Macao et Cosmage* © Edy Legrand, 1919. **20** Babar the Elephant © Jean de Brunhoff. **21** *Tim to the Rescue* text and illustrations copyright © Edward Ardizzone, 1949 and reproduced with permission of Frances Lincoln Ltd. **22** *Captain Slaughterboard Drops Anchor* copyright © Mervyn Peake. **23** *High Street* by J M Richards. Illustrations copyright © Eric Ravillious 1938. Published by Egmont UK Ltd London and used with permission. **24 (top)** *The Arabs* copyright © The estate of Edward Bawden; **(bottom)** *Orlando's Invisible Pyjamas* copyright © Kathleen Hale, 1947 and reproduced by permission of Frederick Warne & Co. **25 (top)** *The Little White Bear* copyright © Enid Marx, 1945; **(bottom)** *Village and Town*, by Stanley Badmin, 1947 and reproduced by permission of Penguin Books Ltd. **26** *Mary Belinda and the Ten Aunts* copyright © Susan Einzig and reproduced with kind permission of Hetty Einzig and Mary Kuper. **27** *Little Red Engine Goes to Town* text by Diana Ross, Illustrations © Leslie Wood, 1952. **28** *Sparkle and Spin* © Paul Rand, 1957. **29** *See and Say* © DACS 2011. **30** *Little Blue and Little Yellow* © Leo Lionni, 1962. **31** *Les Larmes de Crocodile* or *Crocodile Tears* © Andre Francois, 1956. **32** *Old Winkle and the Seagulls*; copyright © Gerald Rose, 1960. **33 (top)** Illustrations from *Birds* by Brian Wildsmith, copyright © Brian Wildsmith, 1980, reprinted by permission of Oxford University Press; **(bottom)** Illustrations from *A Child's Garden of Verse* by Brian Wildsmith, copyright © Brian Wildsmith, 1966, reprinted by permission of Oxford University Press. **34** Illustrations for *Railway Passage* and *Adam and Paradise Island* by Charles Keeping © B.L. Kearley Ltd. **35** *Humbert* by John Burningham, published by Jonathan Cape, used by permission of The Random House Group Ltd. **36** *Goggles* © Ezra Jack Keats, 1969. **37** *The Tiger Who Came to Tea*, © Judith Kerr, 1968. **38–39** *This is London*, © Miroslav Sasek, 1959. **40** *Where the Wild Things Are* by Maurice Sendak, copyright © Maurice Sendak, 1963, published by Bodley Head, used by permission of The Random House Group Ltd. **41** *The Favershams* by Roy Gerrard, copyright © Roy Gerrard 1982, and reproduced by permission of Penguin Books Ltd. **42** © Cai Gao. **43** *When the Moon Forgot* © Jimmy Liao, 2009. **44** Image from *The Arrival* by Shaun Tan (2006), reproduced with permission from Lothian Books, an imprint of Hachette Australia. U.S. edition published by Arthur A. Levine Books, an imprint of Scholastic Inc. **45** *Little Tree* © Kastumi Komagata, 2008, reproduced with kind permission from the artist. **46 (top)** *La Visite de Petite Mort* © Kitty Crowther 2004, reproduced with permission from the publisher, L'école des Loisirs. **46 (bottom)** *Obax* text and illustrations © André Neves 2010, published with permission from Brinque-Book, São Paulo, Brazil. **48** *Petit Robert et la Mystère du*

Frigidaire copyright © Fabian Negrin. **51** *The Model and her Reflection*, lithograph © Edward Ardizzone, 1955. Permission granted by the Artist's Estate. **52** Illustration from *One, Five Many* by Kveta Patkovska. Copyright © Kveta Patkovska, 1990, reproduced with kind permission from the artist. **53 (top)** *The Cats Go to Market* text © Joan E. Cass and illustration © William Stobbs, 1969; **(bottom)** *Off to Windmill Hill* copyright © The Estate of Edward Bawden. **54** Cover of *The Shape of Content* © Estate of Ben Shahn/DACS, London/ VAGA, New York 2011. **55 & 57** Sketchbook pages © Merja Palin, Karen Thompson, Antoaneta Ouzounova and Kathrin Lang, all reproduced with kind permission from the artists. **58** Alexis Deacon sketchbook images copyright © Alexis Deacon. **60–61** *Last Summer by the Seaside* by Andrew Gordon © Andrew Gordon, 2009. **62–65** *Manu is Feeling…From A to Z* by Madelena Moniz © Madelena Moniz, reproduced with kind permission from the artist. **66–69** *Un Lion à Paris* © Beatrice Alemagna, 2006. **70–72** *Robinson Crusoe* © Ajubel, 2008 & © Media Vaca, 2008. **74** *Zoo* by Anthony Browne, copyright © Anthony Browne 1992, published by Red Fox. Used by permission of The Random House Group Ltd. **76** *The Stinky Cheese Man*, Lane Smith. Artwork © Lane Smith 1992. Text ©Jon Scieszka 1992. **78–79** *Lily Takes a Walk*, copyright © Satoshi Kitamura, reproduced with kind permission from the artist. **82** *The Tunnel* written and illustrated by Anthony Browne. Illustrations © 1989 Anthony Browne. Reproduced by permission of Walker Books Ltd, London SE11 5HJ. **83** © Lauren Child, 2002. **84** One double page spread from *The Frog Prince Continued* by Jon Scieszka and illustrated by Steve Johnson (Puffin, 1991, 1992, 1994). Text copyright © Jon Scieszka, 1991. Illustrations copyright © Steve Johnson, 1991. **88–89** *Come away from the Water, Shirley* by John Burningham, copyright © John Burningham, published by Jonathan Cape. Used by permission of The Random House Group Ltd. **92–93** *Owl Babies* written by Martin Waddell and illustrated by Patrick Benson. Illustrations © 1992 Patrick Benson. Reproduced by permission of Walker Books Ltd, London SE11 5HJ. **94** *Rosie's Walk* by Pat Hutchins, copyright © Pat Hutchins, published by Bodley Head. Used by permission of The Random House Group Ltd. **95** *I Hate My Teddy Bear* © David McKee, 1982. First Published in Great Britain in 1982 by Andersen Press Limited, London. **96** *Granpa* by John Burningham, copyright © John Burningham, published by Jonathan Cape. Used by permission of The Random House Group Ltd. **97** *Clown* by Quentin Blake, copyright © Quentin Blake, published by Jonathan Cape. Used by permission of The Random House Group Ltd. **98–99** *Um Dia Na Praia* © 2008, Planeta Tangerina © Bernardo Carvalho. **100** *The Mouse's Tale* © Lewis Carroll, 1865. **101** *My First Nursery Book* by Franciszka Thermerson, copyright © Franciszka Thermerson 1946, reproduced with permission from Tate Publishing Ltd. **102** *The Heart in the Bottle* written and illustrated by Oliver Jeffers, copyright © Oliver Jeffers 2010, reproduced by kind permission of the artist. **103** *The Great Paper Caper* written and illustrated by Oliver Jeffers, copyright © Oliver Jeffers 2008, reproduced by kind permission of the artist. **104–105** *Hip Hop Dog*, written by Chris Raschka and Illustrated and designed by Vladimir Radunsky. **106** *Pink Piglet*, text © Marcin Brykcynski, illustration © Joanna Olech, layout © Marta Ignerska, 2006 reproduced with permission from Winged Chariot Press. **108–110** *No!* written and illustrated by Marta Altés. © Marta Altés, 2010 martaltes.com. **112** *Bully* by David Hughes. Illustrations © 1992 David Hughes. Reproduced by permission of Walker Books Ltd, London SE11 5HJ. **114–115** *Mare en de Dingen*, text copyright © Tine Mortier, illustration copyright © Kaatje Vermeire, book copyright © De Eenhoorn Publishers. Reproduced with kind permission from the De Eenhoorn Publishers. **116–117** *Sinna Mann*, picturebook by Gro Dahle (writer) and Svein Nyhus (illustrator), Cappelen, Oslo, Norway 2003. **118–119** *Håret Til Mamma*, picturebook by Gro Dahle (writer) and Svein Nyhus (illustrator), Cappelen, Oslo, Norway 2007. **120–121** *Welhavens Vase* by Bjørn Rune Lie copyright © Bjørn Rune Lie and reproduced with kind permission from the artist. **122–123** *Death, Duck and the Tulip* © Wolf Erlbruch, Verlag Antje Kunstmann GmbH, München 2007. English version Gecko Press, New Zealand 2007. **124** *Blue Bird* © Sunkyung Cho 2005, reproduced with

kind permission from the artist. **125** *The Sad Book* written by Michael Rosen and illustrated by Quentin Blake. Illustrations © Quentin Blake, 2004. Reproduced by permission of Walker Books Ltd, London SE11 5HJ. **126–127** © Armin Greder, 2008. **128 (top)** *The Conquerors* © David McKee, 2004. First published in Great Britain 2004 by Andersen Press Limited, London; **(bottom)** *Tusk Tusk* © David McKee, 1978. First published in Great Britain 1978 by Andersen Press Limited, London. **129–130** *Jij Lievert*, text © Geert De Kockere, illustrations © Sabien Clement and book © De Eenhoorn Publishers, 2002. **131 & 134** *The Journey* by Lee Kow Fong, images © Lee Kow Fong 2010, reproduced with kind permission of the artist. **132–133** Illustrations by Becky Palmer, images © Rebecca Palmer 2010, reproduced with kind permission of the artist. **136 (bottom)** *The Old Print Room* drawing by Hannah Webb, © Hannah Webb, reproduced with kind permission from the artist. **137** *Rain and Hail*, illustrations © Helen Borten, 1963. **138** *Treasure Island* illustrated by John Lawrence. Illustrations © 2009 John Lawrence. Reproduced by permission of Walker books Ltd, London SE11 5HJ. **139 (left)** *The Sixpence that Rolled Away* © The Estate of Edward Bawden; **(right)** *Toy Car* cardboard print by Chloë Cheese, reproduced with kind permission from the artist. **140** *Liefde kan niet zonder liefde* text © Pieter van Oudheusden, illustration © Kevin Van Wonterghem, book © De Eenhoorn Publishers. **141** *Voorspel van een gebroken liefde* text © Geert De Kockere, illustration © Isabelle Vandenabeele, book © De Eenhoorn Publishers. **142** *The Haunted House* text and illustration © Kazuno Kohara, reproduced with kind permission from the artist. **143** *Red Light Green Light* ©Andrew Kulman, reproduced with kind permission from the artist. **144** *Chain of Happiness* screenprint © Marta Altés, 2010, reproduced with kind permission from the artist. **145–146** *Mannetje en Vrouwtje krijgen een kind* text © Brigitte Minne, illustration © Kaatje Vermeire, book © De Eenhoorn Publishers. **147** *The Little Red Fish* © Tae-Eun Yoo 2007. **148** *Red Striped Pants* © Lee Jina. Originally published by Borim Press, Korea 2007. **149 (top)** *Somebody Great Loves Me* monoprints © Suzanne Chim, reproduced with kind permission from the artist; **(bottom)** From *Not Me!*, illustrations copyright © Nicola Killen 2010. Published by Egmont UK Ltd and used with permission. **150** *Cockadoodledon't!* © Mike Smith, reproduced with kind permission from the artist. **151–152** *Gelati in Venice* © Liz Loveless. **153–155** *Star Gazers, Skyscrapers and Extraordinary Sausages* © 2010 Claudia Boldt boldt@cloudcukoostudio.com. Reproduced by kind permission of Child's Play (International) Ltd. **156–157** Gwénola Carrère, *ABC Cercasi*, © Topipittori.www.topipittori.it. **158–159** Monotypes copyright © Yann Kebbi, reproduced with kind permission from the arist. **160–161** *On va au parc!* Author of the text and the illustrations Fabian Negrin. **164 & 186** *It's a Book* text and artwork © Lane Smith 2010. **166** *How to Catch a Star* written and illustrated by Oliver Jeffers, copyright © Oliver Jeffers 2005, reproduced by kind permission of the artist. **169** *Mr Peek and the Misunderstanding at the Zoo* by Kevin Waldron. Cover design by Kevin Waldron and Mike Jolley, published by Templar Publishing. **170** *The Princess Blankets* written by Carol Ann Duffy, paintings (illustration) by Catherine Hyde. Cover Design by Janie Louise Hunt, published by Templar Publishing. **173** *Good Little Wolf* storyboard © Nadia Shireen, reproduced with kind permission from the artist. **174–175** *Good Little Wolf* by Nadia Shireen, published by Jonathan Cape. Reprinted by permission of The Random House Group Ltd. **176–177** Courtesy Thierry Magnier. **178 (right) & 179** *No Hay Tiempo para Jugar* text © Sandra Arenal, 2004, illustrations © Mariana Chiesa, 2004, published by Media Vaca, 2004. **180** *Libro de las Preguntas* text © Pablo Neruda and illustrations © Isidro Ferrer, published by Media Vaca. **181** Joanna Concejo, "L'angelo Delle Scarpe", © 2009 Topipittori. www.topipittori.it. **182** Beatrice Alemagna, "Che Cos'e Un Bambino", © 2008 Topipittori. www. topipittori.it. **183 (top)** *Rood Rood Roodkapje* text © Edward van de Vendel, illustrations © Isabelle Vandenabeele, book © De Eenhoorn Publishers; **(bottom)** *Het geheim van de keel van de nachtegaal*, text © Peter Verhelst, illustrations © Carll Cneut, book © De Eenhoorn Publishers. **184** Courtesy WingedChariot.